# The Black Farmer Cookbook

Wilfred Emmanuel-Jones

# Black Farmer

Cookbook

Wilfred Emmanuel-Jones

Food and reportage photography by Steve Lee

**SIMON & SCHUSTER**

A CBS COMPANY

First published in Great Britain
by Simon & Schuster UK Ltd. 2009
A CBS Company

Simon & Schuster UK Ltd
1st Floor
222 Gray's Inn rd
London
WC1X 8HB

*Managing Editor:* Paula Borton
*Design:* Jane Humphrey
*Food and reportage photography:*
Steve Lee

1 3 5 7 9 10 8 6 4 2

Printed and bound in China

ISBN 978-1-84737-394-6

# CONTENTS

Writing this book has given me the opportunity to go back in time and revisit various stages of my life. As a boy, the cards were stacked heavily against me doing something worthwhile with my future. As a first-generation child from parents who came to this country in the 1950s, life was a struggle. I knew what it was like to be poor and hungry.

Completing this book is a great personal achievement because I am a product of one of those schools that can more often than not perpetuate a pupil's sense of failure and hopelessness. There wasn't much expected of the kids at my school. The system seemed to be processing children destined for society's rubbish heap. It seemed everybody hated being at my school – the pupils and the teachers.

On this trip down memory lane: age eleven, I was such a difficult child. At school I made my teachers' lives hell. My situation back then was one of confusion and despair. I owe everything that I have subsequently achieved to a very particular friend – a dream.

My dream helped me through the dark and seemingly hopeless period of growing up. Whatever problems life threw at me, this dream was a comforting corner where I could go and lick my wounds. It was a friend who gave encouragement when all around was cynicism and criticism; who offered hope when all around was despair; who guided me back on track when I deviated. Whatever was going on with my life there was one safe place to go.

Although I was brought up in inner-city Birmingham, my father had an allotment that it was my responsibility to look after. It was while working on my father's allotment that I first met my friend. My dream offered space, freedom, hope and self-worth. It led me to believe that my purpose in life was to have a farm of my own, and the only way I was going to achieve that was to make a friend of the dream that one day I would.

I kept faithfully to my dream and it took me nearly forty years before I bought my own farm. So I thank young Wilfred for possessing the courage to have a dream in the first place and the will and focus to stay loyal to it.

The journey I took to achieve my dream led me into the world of food. First I trained and worked as a chef, plying my trade in various hamburger joints, restaurants and hotels – the unglamorous end of the business. From there I worked in television as a director, travelling the world making programmes about food and drink. As a director I had the pleasure of working with some of today's top chefs before they were on anyone's radar: the likes of Gordon Ramsay, who gave me the pleasure of cooking Sunday lunch, Antony Worrall Thompson, Jean Christophe Novelli, Brian Turner, Raymond Blanc, to name a few. After a career in television, in an urgent attempt to earn enough money to buy my farm, I set up my own food and drink marketing agency where I worked with some of the most innovative brands of the last decade, ranging from Cobra beer and Loyd Grossman sauces to KETTLE® Chips and Plymouth gin.

Thankfully that business was a success and some ten years ago I was at last able to buy my own small farm. That in turn set alight another great passion of mine – a love of rural Britain and in particular the people of the West Country.

In writing this book I have tried to give you the story behind many of my recipes. It is a book that I hope you will be able to sit down and read, not just for the recipes but also to discover the motivation that led to the dishes.

Food is the engine room of living life; it is so important that in some places it is worshipped, in others it is treated as an art form and, for me, it has been the device to take me down memory lane.

The memories of shopping jaunts with my mother, or all eight of my brothers and sisters sitting around the table on Sundays desperate to tuck into chicken with rice and peas, are enough to start me cooking. Eating the first lamb that I reared had a lot of significance because there is nothing more gratifying than producing food from field to fork.

I have always believed that you don't achieve the things you want in life on your own. If you work hard and focus, the people you need to help you on your life's journey are somehow sent to help you achieve your goal. I must thank my wife Michaela. She had the courage to share my ambition and worked almost beyond human endurance to help achieve my dream of owning a farm. Her mind for detail and her encouragement have put this manuscript into a state that I could send to the publisher. Kim Morphew has worked tirelessly on the recipes and got them to a stage that makes them easy to follow. I must also thank Paula Borton and Janet Copleston at Simon and Schuster for approaching me to write this book – you will never know how that faith in me has set a few demons to rest.

I must thank the Harris family from Rhiwlas Farm, Raglan, in Monmouthshire: they may not know this, but when, some twenty years ago, their daughter Caroline rolled up with me in tow to spend Christmas with them on their farm it proved an important tonic that kept me on track to achieve my dream. Apart from having to manage the shock of dealing with this ruffian that their daughter had dragged in from the streets, Caroline's mum, Elsie, showed great kindness and hospitality that gave me the faith to keep going.

Finally I have to thank my next-door neighbours Chris and Carole Budge, who have shown nothing but patience and kindness ever since I bought my farm. Chris manages the farm and without his help and guidance it would never be able to function. I rely on him to maintain the place. He does all the hard work and I remain eternally grateful to him.

So all that is left for me to say is that I hope you enjoy my journey as much as I have in telling it and you take away one message: The Black Farmer® is passionate about flavour! I believe that flavour should not be confined by tradition, but should be the result of the bringing together of interesting ingredients that produce truly distinctive recipes.

# LAMB
## AND MUTTON

Lamb for me is not just one of my favourite meats: it was these fine creatures that helped me fulfil my lifelong dream of becoming a farmer. My first small flock gave me those vital credentials. They taught me some of the most important lessons I have ever learnt about the role of the farmer in our society and shaped my views and opinions on the state of farming in this country.

So, for starters, share with me this, the first time I prepared one of my lambs for lunch – Classic Roast Leg of Lamb. A special meal like this demands a special occasion, and the friends who had started with me on my farming journey were invited to join me to celebrate this momentous day. **I have cooked roast lamb hundreds of times but this was different.** It was an experience that has stayed with me despite it having happened more than ten years ago. I can remember every detail about that day as if it were yesterday, and as I prepared this particular leg of lamb for roasting I knew that I was paying homage to a very special joint. The occasion demanded reverence.

On that day, all the ingredients that would go into making this dish had to be the best and prepared with care. It's as though all my senses had realized the significance of this meal and had become heightened in readiness. To this day I have not smelt garlic and rosemary as fresh and pungent as those on that May afternoon down on my farm. As I take myself back to that day I can conjure up the mouth-watering aroma of the joint of lamb. It looked and smelt like no other before or since. It was larger than I would normally get from the butcher or supermarket. There was a more generous amount of fat around the leg than I had been used to and the colour, oh the colour! It was a beautiful pinky red that shone freshness, a freshness that demanded that I prepare an unforgettable meal. This joint tasted better than any I have ever eaten, and my friends concurred. It completed a circle for me; I had a sense not only of satisfaction in preparing such a tasty meal but also of a great achievement. As I lay in the sun preparing for a doze I knew that today would forever be etched on my memory. This meal was a product of my labour that went way beyond the cooking stage. This joint was from a lamb that I had reared myself, my very first 'from field to plate' experience.

# CLASSIC ROAST LEG OF LAMB

This simple recipe is a great way to enjoy sweet and tender Broadwoodwidger lamb. Serve with crispy roast parsnips, steamed carrots and peas for the perfect Sunday roast.

**serves 4–6**

**1.65 kg leg of lamb**
**4 fat garlic cloves, cut into slivers**
**6 fresh rosemary sprigs, each cut into 3 pieces**
**50 g can anchovies in oil, drained**
**2 x 410 g cans cannellini beans, drained and rinsed**
**200 ml dry white wine**
**2 tablespoons plain flour**
**300 ml lamb stock**
**salt and freshly ground black pepper**

1. Preheat the oven to Gas Mark 5/190°C/fan oven 170°C. Take a small knife and, using the tip, make about 12 incisions all over the leg of lamb. Into each incision insert a sliver of garlic, a small sprig of rosemary and an anchovy fillet, pushing them right down into the incision. You can use the end of a spoon to help push the bits in.

2. Season the joint well and place in a roasting tin – any leftover rosemary sprigs can be placed under the joint for more flavour. Roast in the oven for about 1 hour 30 minutes, basting the joint during roasting.

3. Remove the roasting tin from the oven and add the cannellini beans and white wine. Return to the oven for a further 15–20 minutes for medium or a little longer until cooked to your liking (see tip). Remove the lamb from the tin and put onto a carving board. Loosely cover with foil and set aside for 15 minutes.

4. Meanwhile, with a slotted spoon, transfer the cannellini beans to a serving dish and keep warm. Discard the rosemary sprigs and place the roasting tin on the hob. Sprinkle over the flour and cook for 30 seconds, scraping up any residue in the bottom of the tin. Gradually add the stock, whisking until smooth, and bring to the boil. Bubble for a few minutes until thickened. Check the seasoning.

5. Carve the lamb into slices by cutting diagonally from the knuckle end. Serve with the cannellini beans and gravy.

**tip** If you prefer your lamb less pink, then cook it for an extra 25 minutes in step 2.

# SPICY THAI LAMB SALAD

This is a mouth-watering recipe that is ideal with deliciously pink lamb left over from a roast, or see the tip on how to make from scratch – the only extra time is cooking the lamb, which takes minutes.

**serves 4**

125 g rice noodles
2 tablespoons sesame oil
150 g cherry tomatoes, halved
a small handful of fresh coriander, finely chopped
a small handful of fresh mint, finely chopped
1 small red onion, finely sliced
150 g bean sprouts
115 g bag leafy salad with tatsoi
¼ cucumber, deseeded and sliced in moons
about 400 g leftover roast lamb, thinly sliced
salt and freshly ground black pepper

**for the dressing**
1 teaspoon dark brown sugar
juice of 2 limes
1 red chilli, deseeded and finely sliced
2 teaspoons fish sauce
2 tablespoons light soy sauce
1 tablespoon sesame oil
1 garlic clove, finely chopped

1. Put the rice noodles into a large bowl and cover with boiling water. Set aside for 5 minutes, or according to pack instructions, until tender. Drain, rinse in cold water and drain again. Toss with the sesame oil and set aside.
2. Mix all the ingredients for the dressing together. Check for seasoning (if you would like it sweeter add a little more sugar, if you'd like it hotter add a little more chilli).
3. When ready to serve, put the cherry tomatoes, coriander, mint, red onion, bean sprouts, salad leaves and cucumber into a large bowl. Season. Add the noodles and dressing and toss to coat.
4. Divide the salad between four plates and top each with the sliced lamb. Serve immediately.

**tip** To make from scratch, season 500 g chunky lamb leg steaks with salt and pepper and rub in 2 tablespoons of olive oil. Heat a heavy-based frying pan and sear the lamb on all sides for about 3–4 minutes per side. You will need to do this in batches. Set aside and loosely cover with foil for 5 minutes. Then thinly slice and add to the salad at step 4.

My farming journey started on New Year's Day 2002, a cold winter's day. I had a house full of friends up from London to celebrate Christmas and New Year. It is amazing how popular you become during the holiday season when you have a nice big farmhouse and lovely animals to visit. After a rather drunken evening dancing to the tunes of our youth, we saw the New Year in and eventually hit the sack by 3 a.m. But while everyone was looking forward to a long morning lie-in to recover from the night before I could hardly sleep. I was looking forward to buying my first flock of sheep from the local market.

Looking back, God knows what the locals must have thought of this group of twenty 'up-country' folk, looking totally out of place in the market with their brand-new mud-free wellies. I am sure we were the butt of many a joke that morning, yet they received us with good grace. Along with dear friends Stephen and Valou Byfield and Ray and Sarah Barrett we still enjoy the memory of that momentous day.

That day I bought twenty-four Suffolk lambs and, I tell you, like a proud parent, I thought they were the best-looking lambs in the whole of Britain. Most importantly, as far as I was concerned, their purchase meant I was now a bona fide farmer. Not only a bone fide farmer but one who had twenty hungry friends to feed, whose hunger pangs were all the more acute thanks to fresh country air and massive hangovers. A recipe that I recommend when catering for a large number of people is Lamb and Mint Burgers (page 19). Very easy to make, this is one dish where too many cooks will not spoil the broth.

# LAMB AND MINT BURGERS

These delicious burgers can be cooked on a ridged cast-iron grill on the stove or, when the weather's fine and the coals glowing, on the barbecue outside. Serve these burgers in ciabatta rolls, with mayonnaise, shredded lettuce and sliced tomatoes and relishes on the side.

serves 4

500 g lean lamb mince
1 garlic clove, crushed
½ red onion, finely chopped
3 tablespoons finely chopped fresh mint
50 g semi-dried tomatoes in oil, drained and
   finely chopped
salt and freshly ground black pepper

1. Combine all the ingredients well in a large bowl. Using wet hands, divide the mixture into four and shape into patties. Chill for at least 1 hour.
2. Heat a grill or barbecue to hot and cook the burgers for about 5–6 minutes on each side until starting to char but still a little bit pink in the middle. (Cook for 2–3 minutes longer if you don't want your burgers pink.) Serve immediately with plantain chips (see tip).

tip To make plantain chips, cut peeled plantain into 1 cm thick slices. Heat vegetable oil in a deep-fat fryer or a large saucepan until it is 180°C. Cook for 1–2 minutes, in batches, until golden brown and crispy. Drain on kitchen paper and season before serving.

# LEMON AND BAY LAMB KEBABS

The lemon and bay leaves give these kebabs a definite flavour of Greece. When cooked, squeeze over more lemon juice and a little olive oil.

serves 4

3 tablespoons olive oil
juice of 1 lemon plus 1 large lemon, cut into 8 slices
2 garlic cloves, finely chopped
1 tablespoon finely chopped fresh rosemary
8 fresh bay leaves
900 g boneless leg of lamb, cut into large chunks
1 large red onion, cut into 8 wedges
1 red pepper, deseeded and cut into 8 pieces
1 green pepper, deseeded and cut into 8 pieces
salt and freshly ground black pepper

1. Put the olive oil, lemon juice, garlic, rosemary, bay leaves and seasoning into a large freezer bag. Add the lamb chunks and seal the bag. Massage the lamb through the bag until the lamb is thoroughly coated in the marinade. Leave to marinate for at least 1 hour or up to 8 hours.
2. Thread the lamb, onion and peppers alternately on eight metal or soaked wooden skewers, with a slice of lemon and a bay leaf somewhere in the middle.
3. Brush the skewers with any remaining marinade. Heat a ridged grill pan or fire up the barbecue. Cook the skewers for 5–6 minutes on each side until slightly charred and still a little pink in the middle. Serve immediately.

' There is something special about cooking on a barbecue. From the ritual of preparing and lighting the coals to the sizzling smoky aromas and the chargrilled flavour of the food. It evokes memories of hot summers, making easy barbecue food simply addictive. '

Rearing my own sheep has made me a bit of an evangelist, preaching the wonderful taste of British lamb. Far superior in my view to New Zealand lamb. I was determined to share my meat with food lovers, people interested in meat from happy lambs. I did not want to sell them to the local abattoir for a dead weight and not know where the meat would end up. I wanted people to know that they were eating The Black Farmer lamb. Reared with love and care.

I had a plan. I would get a website and sell online. I rang all of my family and friends and got them to tell all their family and friends that The Black Farmer lamb would be available. As a marketing man I know how important packaging is, so I shelled out for some smart labels and recipe cards and spent a fortune on some fancy carrier bags. Then I thought I would test the idea – slaughtering just one of my lambs to start with.

Having had one of my sheep slaughtered, it then became a race against time to make sure I had enough customers. I had to ring around to find out who would want to buy which cuts. The next three days were the most disappointing as I came to realize why it is so difficult for mail-order meat businesses to make a living selling online. I will have some chops – chump or cutlet? I don't mind as long as it is chops. What about some shoulder? No, chops will do. What about a crown? There are only two of us, all I need is some chops. What about a nice leg? No, we only have leg occasionally. And there is the rub. Everyone wanted the same cut and I was left with the rest of the carcass – I couldn't sell the other cuts for love nor money.

There are a lot of lovely cuts of lamb, but few of my family and friends know what to do with them. Eating habits in this country have changed so much that cuts that I had grown up with were too big for most families, or had so fallen out of favour that people were at a loss as to what to do with them. I was left with a freezer full of The Black Farmer lamb for a good six months from that one lamb, and a lot of the cuts were given away. When it came to the time for the rest of my lambs to be slaughtered I did what all my neighbours had been doing for years: sold them for a price far lower than I could have got if I had sold direct to the consumer. Worse still, I didn't know where the meat was going. For all I know it may have ended up as a minced pulp in a doner kebab shop. What a waste. I am still smarting from that experience, so here is a diagram of a lamb carcass and a description of where the cuts come from and the best cooking methods.

**LEG** Available as a whole or half leg and boneless. Ideal for roasting, such as Classic Roast Leg of Lamb (page 15) and braising as a whole piece, but can be cut into steaks or cubes, which are good for grilling, frying or barbecuing. See Lemon and Bay Lamb Kebabs (page 19).

**FLANK** Located above the breast this is usually used for mince. See Lamb and Mint Burgers (page 19), Lamb Meatballs (page 32) or Shepherd's Pie (page 28).

**BREAST** This is very underrated and provides a perfect and economical slow roast when boned, stuffed and rolled. Cook at about Gas Mark 3/160°C/ fan oven 140°C for 45 minutes per 500 g.

**SHOULDER** The shoulder is often sold as two separate joints but you can buy the whole shoulder, which is called a square and consists of the arm blade and rib bone. Suitable for roasting whole like the Roast Leg of Mutton with Juniper and Thyme (page 39) or cut into chunks for stews or casseroles such as Mediterranean Lamb Casserole (page 26) or Curried Mutton (page 38).

**NECK** This is one of the toughest cuts and is best used for stewing. You can buy middle neck chops, which are perfect for Scotch Broth (page 26) or Lancashire Hot Pot (page 32). The neck has a lot of flavour but you must be prepared to cook this cut for a very long time.

**SCRAG** The meat from this end is usually much fatter and is best used for stews or casseroles.

**BEST END** This is also known as a rack of lamb and is a very tender premium cut. Try Roast Rack of Spicy Lamb with Aubergine Relish (page 33). It is often cut into cutlets; when the bone is removed the cutlets become noisettes, perfect little rounds of tender lamb.

**SHANK** This is an extremely flavoursome part of the lamb but to get the best out of this section you are going to have to cook it very slowly in a stew or braised dish. See Braised Lamb Shanks with Spring Vegetables (page 23).

**LOIN** This is the tenderest part of the lamb, a bit like the sirloin of beef, and is where loin chops are cut from. Perfect for grilling or barbecuing, why not try Moroccan Spiced Lamb Chops with Fruity Couscous (page 34)? However, it is also a great roasting joint, known as the saddle when two loin joints are still joined together.

**CHUMP** This is like the rump of beef and produces great chops perfect for braising, grilling or frying.

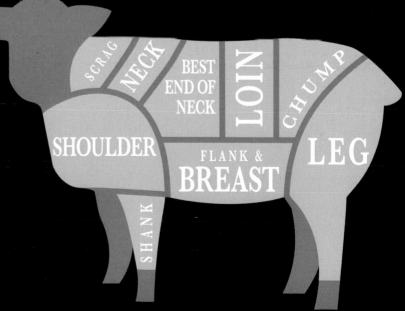

The demands of modern living mean that people can't spend as much time in the kitchen as they would like. The consequence of this is that the tender cuts of meat, which take less time to cook, are more popular, but I find that the more flavoursome parts of the carcass are the cuts that take much longer to cook. I do think it is well worth trying these tasty, warming recipes when you have a little more time on your hands.

# BRAISED LAMB SHANKS
## with Spring Vegetables

There is nothing better and more full of flavour than eating with the seasons. Springtime veggies are a great addition to this light stew, and the shanks provide a great-tasting liquor and melt-in-the-mouth meat. All you need are some boiled new potatoes, ideally Jersey royals.

**serves 4**

50 g butter
1 tablespoon sunflower oil
4 lamb shanks
1 onion, chopped
2 tablespoons plain flour
150 ml dry martini
600 ml chicken stock
175 g baby turnips, scrubbed and trimmed
150 g baby Chantenay carrots, scrubbed and
    trimmed
1 leek, thickly sliced
100 g fine asparagus, trimmed and halved
100 g fresh peas
1 tablespoon chopped fresh parsley
1 tablespoon chopped fresh mint
salt and freshly ground black pepper

1. Heat the butter and oil in a large lidded flameproof casserole pan. Cook the lamb shanks for 5 minutes, turning until brown all over. You will have to do this in batches. Remove and set aside.
2. Add the onion and cook for 3–4 minutes until softened. Stir in the flour and cook for 1 minute, then gradually pour in the martini and stock until smooth and combined.
3. Return the lambs shanks to the pan, season generously and bring to the boil. Cover and simmer for 1 hour. Add the turnips and carrots to the pan. Replace the lid and continue to simmer for 25 minutes or until the lamb falls off the bone and the vegetables are tender.
4. Stir in the leek, asparagus and peas. Simmer for 2–3 minutes until just tender. Check the seasoning and sprinkle over the parsley and mint. Serve immediately.

# SCOTCH BROTH

This is an old-fashioned recipe, great to have on hand when it's freezing cold outside and you need something warm and comforting inside. Make it the day before, for an even tastier punch! It uses middle neck chops, which are unpopular because they can be very tough, but the long cooking produces tender meat with an intense flavour.

serves 4–6

1.25 kg middle neck lamb chops, excess fat trimmed
60 g pearl barley
2 dried bouquet garni sachets
2 carrots, diced
300 g swede, diced
1 leek, sliced
2 tablespoons chopped fresh parsley
salt and freshly ground black pepper

1. Put the lamb chops, pearl barley and bouquet garni in a large saucepan. Season well and pour over 2 litres of cold water. Bring to the boil and then simmer gently for 1 hour, skimming off any scum that rises to the surface.
2. Add the carrots, swede, leek and 600 ml boiling water. Bring back to the boil and simmer for a further 30 minutes or until the vegetables and meat are tender. Remove from the heat and, using a slotted spoon, transfer the lamb chops to a plate. Leave to cool slightly.
3. When cool enough to handle, strip the meat off the bones and tear into bite-size pieces. Carefully scoop off any excess fat from the surface of the broth and discard. Return the shredded lamb to the broth and check seasoning. Gently reheat if necessary, then ladle into bowls and scatter over the parsley. Serve immediately.

# MEDITERRANEAN LAMB CASSEROLE

This is perfect for chilly winter days after a long walk. As with most stews, it improves if made the day before and freezes beautifully – leave out the spinach and Feta and add after reheating. Serve with buttered egg noodles.

serves 4–6

3 tablespoons olive oil
800 g boneless shoulder of lamb, cut into chunks
2 onions, thinly sliced
3 garlic cloves, crushed
1 tablespoon dried oregano
2 fresh bay leaves
300 ml lamb stock
400 g can chopped tomatoes
100 ml balsamic vinegar
410 g can chickpeas, drained and rinsed
50 g sultanas
225 g bag young leaf spinach
100 g Feta cheese, crumbled
freshly ground black pepper

1. Preheat the oven to Gas Mark 4/180°C/fan oven 160°C. Heat half the oil in a large, lidded ovenproof pan and cook the lamb for 5 minutes until browned all over. You will have to do this in batches. Remove and set aside.
2. Add the remaining oil to the pan and cook the onions for 5–8 minutes until they begin to soften and brown. Stir in the garlic, oregano and bay leaves and cook for 1 minute. Return the lamb to the pan and add the stock, tomatoes, balsamic vinegar and some black pepper. Bring gently to the boil then cover and cook in the oven for 1¼ hours.
3. Remove the pan from the oven and stir in the chickpeas and sultanas. Return to the oven for a further 15 minutes or until the juices have thickened and the lamb is tender.
4. To serve, remove the pan from the oven and stir in the spinach until wilted. Divide the casserole between shallow bowls and scatter over the Feta. Serve immediately.

# SHEPHERD'S PIE

A twist on the traditional shepherd's pie, I've mashed sweet potatoes with white ones. Not only does this add a sweetness that goes so well with the lamb, the golden topping looks marvellously appetizing. Serve with a simple green salad to cut through the wonderful richness.

serves 4–6

1 tablespoon olive oil
1 large onion, finely chopped
2 carrots, finely diced
2 celery stick, finely diced
2 garlic cloves, crushed
500 g lean lamb mince
75 ml dark Jamaican rum
2 tablespoons Worcestershire sauce
400 g can chopped tomatoes
1 vegetable stock cube
1 tablespoon dried mixed herbs
50 g hard Devonshire goat's cheese, grated
salt and freshly ground black pepper

for the sweet potato mash
750 g floury potatoes, cut into chunks
500 g sweet potatoes, cut into chunks
2 tablespoons milk
25 g butter

1. Heat the oil in a wide lidded deep pan and gently cook the onion, carrots, celery and garlic for 8–10 minutes until soft and translucent, but not brown. Add the lamb mince, breaking it up with a wooden spoon, and cook for 5 minutes until brown.

2. Add the rum and bubble for a few minutes until nearly evaporated. Stir in the Worcestershire sauce, chopped tomatoes, vegetable stock cube and mixed herbs. Season with salt and black pepper and turn the heat down low. Cover tightly with a lid and simmer for 1 hour.

3. Meanwhile, put the potatoes and the sweet potatoes in a large pan of salted water and bring to the boil. Simmer for 20 minutes until tender. Drain thoroughly, return to the pan and mash until smooth. Then stir in the milk and butter until combined. Season generously. Set aside.

4. Preheat the oven to Gas Mark 5/190°C/fan oven 170°C. Spoon the meat mixture into a 1.5 litre ovenproof dish and cover with the potato mash. If you are feeling fancy, why not pipe the mash on the top. Sprinkle with the cheese.

5. Cook in the oven for 30 minutes until golden and bubbling. Serve immediately.

*To make ahead* Prepare as above to the end of step 4. Then cover and chill in the fridge for up to 2 days or freeze. Bring back to room temperature or defrost thoroughly before cooking as above.

' Although it is not fashionable in today's throw-away society, as you will see I like dishes that can be made and kept refrigerated for several days afterwards. '

When I bought my farm I loved the fact that it was a four-hour drive away from London and situated in real farming country, a part of the world that my urban cousins had no interest in. The tourists that do venture near are more often than not just passing through. The A30 provides them with fast access to the coast and they don't even need to stop off at my local town, Launceston, for provisions. Even if they wanted to they would find that most of the shops would be closed by midday on a Saturday.

The real charm of this location is that it belongs to a bygone age. There are positives and negatives to this. At its best there is a sense of community that is the envy of many an urban conurbation. The people are friendly and trustworthy, and people are what matter down here. Our urban cousins have a variety of public services to call on in times of need; if you have a problem in the rural communities you only have each other to rely on.

# LAMB MEATBALLS

This will soon become a family favourite in your house as it has in mine. Make a batch and freeze in individual portions for a really tasty freezer stand-by. Simply defrost before warming in a pan on the hob until piping hot.

**serves 4**

½ onion, finely chopped
1 garlic clove, crushed
zest of ½ lemon
1 teaspoon ground coriander
1 teaspoon ground cumin
500 g lean lamb mince
1 tablespoon olive oil
1 quantity Sweet and Spicy Tomato Sauce
    (see page 177)
salt and freshly ground black pepper

1. In a large bowl mix together the onion, garlic, lemon zest, coriander, cumin and lamb mince. Season generously. With wet hands shape the mixture into 20 small balls.
2. Heat the oil in a non-stick frying pan and cook the meatballs for 5 minutes until brown all over. You will need to do this in batches. Return all the browned meatballs to the pan and pour over the Sweet and Spicy Tomato Sauce. Bring to the boil, cover and simmer for 15 minutes until the meatballs are cooked. Serve immediately.

# LANCASHIRE HOT POT

In our society we are so hung up on low carb or low fat foods that we sometimes forget the truly special things in life. This dish uses chump chops, which are very different from the popular loin chop and much cheaper. For a real extra treat serve with pickled red cabbage on the side. Thanks to Sarah Barrett for letting us use her special family recipe.

**serves 4**

1 tablespoon groundnut oil
900 g chump or middle neck lamb chops
2 onions, finely sliced
1 tablespoon plain flour
600 ml lamb stock
2 tablespoons brown sauce
1 tablespoon mushroom ketchup
1 tablespoon dried thyme
¼ teaspoon ground mixed spice
350 g swede, sliced
500 g sweet potato, sliced
salt and freshly ground black pepper

1. Preheat the oven to Gas Mark 3/160°C/fan oven 140°C. Heat the oil in a frying pan and cook the lamb chops for 5 minutes until browned all over. Remove and transfer to a lidded ovenproof casserole dish.
2. Add the onions to the frying pan and gently cook for 8–10 minutes until softened and starting to brown. Stir in the flour then gradually add the stock until smooth and combined. Stir in the brown sauce, mushroom ketchup, thyme and mixed spice and season generously. Bring to a simmer then pour over the lamb chops in the casserole dish.
3. Arrange the swede and sweet potatoes over the top, overlapping to cover the top of the dish. Cover and cook in the oven for 1½ hours.
4. Remove the lid and cook the hot pot for a further 30–40 minutes until the lamb is tender and the potatoes are starting to brown and crisp. Serve immediately.

Herbs and spices are a great way to add to the flavour of lamb, but not overpower. My love for the exotic has inspired this recipe, offering up a romantic meal for two, a Moorish feast and a twist on classic meatballs that will soon become a family favourite. So prepare your taste buds for a real taste sensation.

## ROAST RACK OF SPICY LAMB
**with Aubergine Relish**

Ask your butcher to French trim the lamb rack or, if you want to do it yourself, carefully scrape down the bone ends using a sharp knife until you reach the meat, removing excess fat.

**serves 2**

400 g rack of lamb, French trimmed
1 quantity Mixed Herb and Chilli Paste (see page 60)

**for the aubergine relish**
3 tablespoons olive oil
1 onion, finely chopped
1 garlic clove, finely chopped
1 aubergine (about 300 g), cut into small cubes
1 teaspoon ground cumin
1 teaspoon ground coriander
3 cardamom pods, seeds removed and crushed
2 tablespoons tomato purée
2 tablespoons chopped fresh coriander

1. Score lightly across the fat on the back of the lamb rack and put into a large freezer bag. Add the Mixed Herb and Chilli Paste and seal the bag. From the outside, massage the paste into the lamb until coated. Set aside in a cool place for 2 hours.

2. Preheat the oven to Gas Mark 6/200°C/fan oven 180°C. Remove the lamb from the freezer bag and put on a roasting tray. Cook in the oven for 20 minutes.

3. Meanwhile make the aubergine relish. Heat the oil in a wide lidded frying pan and gently cook the onion, garlic and aubergine for 5–8 minutes until the onion is soft and the aubergine is starting to brown. Reduce the heat and add the ground cumin, ground coriander and crushed cardamom seeds. Cook for 1 minute, stirring constantly.

4. Stir in the tomato purée and 2 tablespoons water and cook for 30 seconds. Cover and cook on a very low heat for 15 minutes, stirring occasionally, until the aubergine is really soft.

5. Remove the lamb from the oven, loosely wrap in foil and set aside for 10 minutes.

6. To serve, stir the coriander through the aubergine relish and divide between two plates. Carve the lamb into cutlets and place on top of the aubergine relish. Serve immediately.

# MOROCCAN SPICED LAMB CHOPS

**with Fruity Couscous**

This simple recipe is a great way to enjoy sweet and tender lamb chops. The Moroccan spices go so well with the meat it's worth ringing the changes once in a while. I've teamed the chops with couscous, which can be made ahead of time – it heats up beautifully in the microwave.

**serves 4**

1 teaspoon cumin seeds

10 g crystallized rose petals

1 teaspoon ground coriander

½ teaspoon turmeric

½–1 teaspoon chilli flakes, depending on how hot
    you like it

8 lamb loin chops, trimmed of some fat if necessary

salt and freshly ground black pepper


**for the fruity couscous**

225 g dried couscous

25 g butter

300 ml boiling hot chicken stock

1 tablespoon olive oil

200 g super sweet cherry tomatoes, halved

2 teaspoons pomegranate syrup

50 g sultanas

50 g ready-to-eat apricots, chopped

2 fresh mint sprigs, leaves chopped

4 fresh coriander sprigs, leaves chopped

2 fresh flat-leaf parsley sprigs, leaves chopped

25 g pine nuts, toasted

juice of 1 lemon

1. Put the cumin seeds into a mortar and pestle and lightly crush. Add the rose petals, ground coriander, turmeric and chilli flakes and lightly crush. Put the lamb chops into a shallow non-metallic dish and scatter over the crushed spices. Rub all over and set aside. If you have time you can leave these to marinate for up to 8 hours.

2. Put the couscous and butter in a roomy bowl and pour over the stock. Cover with clingfilm and set aside for 10 minutes. Meanwhile, preheat the grill to medium hot.

3. Heat the oil in a frying pan and add the cherry tomatoes. Stir in the pomegranate syrup and cook gently for 2–3 minutes, until the tomatoes have just started to soften. Set aside.

4. Put the lamb chops on a grill pan and cook under the grill for 5–6 minutes on each side or until cooked to your liking.

5. Meanwhile, stir the couscous with a fork to fluff up the grains then stir the sultanas, apricots, chopped herbs and pine nuts into the couscous. Stir in the cherry tomatoes and pan juices and lemon juice. Check the seasoning and keep warm until the lamb is cooked.

6. Serve the chops with a generous helping of the fruity couscous.

At its worst, some of the attitudes that still exist no longer have much currency in wider society. Many country folk will do their utmost to keep away from the large cities and even pride themselves on never setting foot in such places. To them, multicultural Britain is something to be feared and to stay well clear of. I was the first black person that some of my community had ever met and I would have to travel miles before I saw another person of colour.

My colour was what set me apart and for some of my neighbours it was what defined me. It was easiest for them to refer to me as 'the black farmer'. I pride myself on being a person who has never allowed my skin colour to get in the way of what I want to achieve. It had been a hard road travelled to fulfil my dream of owning a farm, so, rather than take offence at the title that my neighbours had bestowed on me, I decided I would wear it with pride and use the name for all my food products.

I can't finish this chapter without giving you some recipes for mutton. I am pleased to say that over the years there has been a growing interest in mutton as an alternative to lamb. Back in the 1960s mutton was a regular in my household. Mutton is from sheep that are more than two years old and as a result has a much darker flesh and a much stronger flavour. Due to the age of the sheep the mutton will be much tougher than lamb, so it takes a good deal longer to cook. But the wonderful flavour is well worth all that extra wait.

## CURRIED MUTTON

This has been inspired by the classic curried goat, but as goat is not readily available mutton makes a great alternative. Serve with lots of boiled basmati rice and a fresh garden salad.

**serves 6**

4 tablespoons sunflower oil

1.25 kg leg or shoulder of mutton, cut into 2.5 cm
   chunks

1 onion, chopped

2 tablespoons tomato purée

2 garlic cloves, crushed

10 g fresh ginger, peeled and grated

6 whole cloves

2 cardamom pods, split

6 whole black peppercorns, lightly crushed

2 tablespoons hot curry powder

¼ teaspoon turmeric

2 teaspoons mild or hot chilli powder

1 tablespoon ground coriander

¼ teaspoon cumin seeds, lightly crushed

3 large tomatoes, chopped

salt

1. Heat half the oil in a large heavy-based pan and fry the mutton chunks for 5 minutes until brown all over. You will have to do this in batches. Remove and set aside. Add the remaining oil and cook the onion for 3–4 minutes until starting to brown.

2. Add the tomato purée, garlic and ginger and cook for 1 minute. Then stir in the cloves, cardamom pods, peppercorns, curry powder, turmeric, chilli powder, coriander and cumin seeds. Season with a little salt. Cook for 1 minute, stirring until the aromas are released.

3. Return the mutton to the pan and stir in the tomatoes and 600 ml water. Bring to the boil and simmer very gently for 1½–2 hours, until the meat is tender and the sauce has thickened. If after 1½ hours the sauce has thickened but the meat is not tender, cover the pan with a lid to prevent the curry drying out, and continue to cook for a further 30 minutes. Serve immediately.

## ROAST LEG OF MUTTON
### with Juniper and Thyme

This method of slow roasting makes the meat tender and juicy. The wine, garlic, juniper and rosemary are Mediterranean touches, so this is really a Roman-influenced recipe.

**serves 12**

3 garlic cloves, peeled
1 tablespoon juniper berries
a small handful of fresh thyme
2 teaspoons salt
75 g butter, softened
3 kg leg of mutton
300 ml red wine
about 300–400 ml hot lamb stock
2 tablespoons plain flour
salt and freshly ground black pepper

1. Preheat the oven to Gas Mark 3/160°C/fan oven 140°C. Put the garlic, juniper berries, thyme and salt into a mortar and pestle and pound until a coarse paste is formed. Transfer to a bowl and mix with the butter.
2. With a sharp knife, score five or six deep cuts across the leg of mutton and push the flavoured butter into the cuts. Put the meat into a roasting tin and pour the red wine over.
3. Cover with a large piece of foil and roast in the oven for 4–4½ hours, basting every hour with the pan juices and removing the foil for the last 30 minutes.
4. Transfer the joint to a board, cover with foil and leave to rest for 15 minutes. Meanwhile, transfer the pan juices to a jug and leave to settle. Discard the fat and then top the juices up to 600 ml with the hot lamb stock.
5. Return the roasting tin to the hob, sprinkle over the flour and cook for 30 seconds, scraping up any residue in the bottom of the tin. Gradually add the reserved juices, whisking until smooth, and bring to the boil. Bubble for a few minutes until thickened then check the seasoning. Carve the lamb into thick slices and serve with the gravy.

## FIERY STUFFED SHOULDER OF MUTTON

This recipe requires a boned shoulder, so if you're not too handy with a sharp knife, ask your butcher to bone it for you.

**serves 6**

150 g old white bread, torn into pieces
2 green finger chillies, chopped
2 tablespoons olive oil
50 g butter
1 onion, finely chopped
2 garlic cloves, crushed
1 tablespoon finely chopped fresh parsley
2 tablespoons finely chopped fresh coriander
zest of 1 lemon
½ teaspoon freshly grated nutmeg
1 egg, beaten
2 kg boned shoulder of mutton
salt and freshly ground black pepper

1. Preheat the oven to Gas Mark 3/160°C/fan oven 140°C. Put the bread pieces into a food processor along with the green chillies and whizz until the bread becomes crumbs and the chilli is finely minced. Transfer to a large bowl.
2. Heat 1 tablespoon of the oil and the butter in a large frying pan and cook the onion and garlic for 3–4 minutes until beginning to soften. Transfer to the breadcrumb mixture along with the parsley, coriander, lemon zest and nutmeg. Season generously and leave to cool. Stir in the egg until it comes together.
3. Unroll the mutton on a clean board and spoon the stuffing along the length. Re-roll the mutton and tie in five or six places with string. If any stuffing comes out, just push it back in. Transfer to a roasting tin and drizzle with the remaining oil.
4. Cover with foil and roast in the oven for 3–3½ hours, basting the mutton occasionally with the pan juices, until tender. Leave to rest for 15 minutes before carving and serving.

# CHICKEN
## AND DUC

Home for me was a very deprived inner-city area – Small Heath in Birmingham. In fact when I was a child living there some forty years ago, it was regarded as one of the poorest areas in Europe. Eleven of us, four brothers, four sisters, myself and my parents, somehow managed to squeeze into a small two-up two-down terraced house. We were always on the bread line, yet when I was a young lad Sunday lunch after church was the most important meal occasion of the week – an occasion to express our gratitude in prayer for the meal that lay in front of us. I felt no gratitude. For me this ritual was torture, exacerbated by the wonderful smell from the food on the table. Every Sunday it was as if the devil himself was tempting me to dare to start the meal before I was given permission.

'May the Lord make us truly thankful. Amen.' This was the final sentence that I eagerly waited to hear. When one of my younger brothers or sisters who were still learning the prayer said Grace, it felt like an eternity. When it was my turn, I would have said it at triple speed! With a rumbling stomach provoked by the tantalizing smell before me it took all of my powers of restraint not to spoil this most sacred of family rituals.

The centrepiece of this homage was the most glorious meal of the week, Jerk Chicken with Rice and Peas. For many people from the Caribbean this is regarded as their national dish, and many black people from

the Caribbean would have been going through this very same ritual. Forty years on, this is the dish that reminds me of growing up in Small Heath. Even though we were dirt poor every Sunday lunch made me feel like one of the richest men in England.

# JERK CHICKEN
## with Rice and Peas

Pigeon peas are also known as gungo peas and have a wonderful sweet flavour. You can find them in any Caribbean shop or in large supermarkets with a good world food section. If you can't find the peas you could use canned kidney beans or black eyed peas instead.

**serves 4**

1 tablespoon groundnut oil
1 chicken, jointed into 8 pieces
1 onion, finely chopped
2 garlic cloves, chopped
2 tablespoons jerk marinade
400 g can chopped tomatoes
200 ml dry white wine
1 chicken stock cube
2 tablespoons chopped fresh coriander

**for the rice and peas**
1 tablespoon groundnut oil
1 red pepper, deseeded and diced
1 green pepper, deseeded and diced
250 g long grain rice, rinsed
1 teaspoon ground allspice
1 tablespoon fresh thyme leaves
50 g creamed coconut
350 ml hot chicken stock
410 g can green pigeon peas, drained and rinsed
salt and freshly ground black pepper

1. Preheat the oven to Gas Mark 6/200°C/fan oven 180°C. For the jerk chicken, heat 1 tablespoon of groundnut oil in a flameproof casserole pan and cook the chicken pieces for 5 minutes, turning until brown. Remove and set aside. You may have to do this in batches. Add the onion and garlic to the pan and cook gently for 3–4 minutes. Stir in the jerk marinade and cook for 1 minute.

2. Return the chicken pieces to the pan and turn to coat in the onion mixture. Stir in the chopped tomatoes, white wine and stock cube. Cover and cook in the oven for 1 hour.

3. After 40 minutes start cooking the rice and peas. Heat 1 tablespoon of groundnut oil in a large lidded saucepan and cook the peppers for 3–4 minutes until starting to soften. Stir in the rice, allspice, thyme, creamed coconut, stock and peas. Cover with a tight-fitting lid and cook on a low heat for 10–15 minutes, until the rice is tender and the stock has been absorbed. Season generously. Serve the rice and peas with the jerk chicken, scattered with coriander.

If Sunday lunch was the big meal occasion of the week, Saturday morning was the time when I had to earn that place at the dinner table. For this was a time that I had to provide a donkey service to my mother as she made her way around the Bull Ring shopping centre in Birmingham. She never headed for the posh indoor shops, she liked the raw, gritty outdoor markets. It was vibrant, the atmosphere exciting and exotic.

Buying food was a ritual that my mother greatly enjoyed. Here she came to buy the kind of foods that she was used to in the Caribbean: salt fish, plantains, ackee, green banana, red snapper, yams, sweet potatoes, bread fruit. For my mother it was like being back in Jamaica. Watching her buy food was a sight to behold. Every inch of the food was inspected with forensic precision. The stallholders were very patient, allowing her an excessive amount of time to inspect her intended purchase. Having decided that the fruit or vegetables were up to her exacting standards then came the bargaining. A bargain had to be had, that was the game, the thrill. The stallholders understood this and they were experts at giving my mother the essential thrill that made her food shopping worthwhile.

The bartering was tough and relentless. Emotive language was key in keeping up the pressure on the stallholders. **'You rob me. You is mean.' 'May de lard strike you down.' 'Ow could you sleep at night?'** After the stallholder and my mother had exhausted their range of such banter a deal would be struck. Making sure his customer would return for her weekly fix of bartering, the stallholder would pop a free plantain, cut of yam or any fruit he had lying around into my mother's bags, sending her off with the smile of a love-struck teenager.

Having bought the fruit, vegetables and fish her purchases were deposited with the donkey. I would more often than not be cursing the gods for making me her first-born son. At the age of twelve I didn't relish the idea of being a beast of burden, but I always knew when my trials were coming to an end – when we headed for the chicken stall.

Unlike the clinical food world that we live in today, back then in the late sixties you could buy whole chicken that had not been gutted and still had their feathers. Chicken was the main meat that was eaten in my household, which is why it remains my favourite meat. Here are a few of my all-time favourite dishes.

# CITRUS ROAST CHICKEN

By covering the chicken with foil and putting liquid in the base of the tin you are literally steaming and roasting the chicken at the same time, which will give you the most succulent chicken ever. Serve with roast potatoes and sliced runner beans.

**serves 4**

75 g butter
3 lemons
1.75 kg whole chicken
1 large fresh rosemary sprig
a small handful of fresh thyme
2 fresh bay leaves
1 celery stick, trimmed and roughly chopped
2 carrots, roughly chopped
1 onion, roughly chopped
1 garlic bulb, cut in half horizontally
125 ml dry sherry
1 tablespoon plain flour
600 ml chicken stock
salt and freshly ground black pepper

1. Preheat the oven to Gas Mark 5/190°C/fan oven 170°C. In a bowl mix together 50 g butter, the grated zest of 2 lemons and seasoning until combined. Using your fingers, loosen the skin from over the chicken breasts, being careful not to rip the skin. Push the lemon butter between the skin and meat until both breasts are covered. You will find it easier to squidge the butter from the skin side downwards. Slice the 2 zested lemons in half and place in the cavity of the chicken along with the rosemary, thyme and bay leaves.

2. Put the celery, carrots, onion and garlic halves into the base of a large roasting tin. Sit the chicken on top and pour over the dry sherry. With the remaining butter liberally grease a large piece of foil and then use to cover the chicken and roasting tin. Roast in the oven for 1 hour.

3. Remove the foil, baste the chicken with the juices and continue to cook for 30 minutes or until the chicken is cooked. To test, push a skewer into the thickest part of the chicken to see if the juices run clear. Transfer to a carving board and loosely cover with foil.

4. Pass the juices from the roasting tin through a sieve into a jug, crushing the vegetables with the back of a spoon. Put the roasting tin on the hob and gently heat. Sprinkle over the flour, scraping up any residue, and then gradually whisk in the sieved juices until combined. Then stir in the chicken stock and bring to the boil. Bubble for a few minutes until thickened. Carve the chicken and serve with the gravy.

# SPRING GREENS AND PANCETTA CHICKEN PARCELS

Stuffing the chicken breasts and wrapping them in greens and pancetta really helps to keep the meat juicy. Delicious served with griddled vegetables and sautéed potatoes.

**serves 4**

**4 large leaves of Savoy cabbage or spring greens**
**200 g ricotta**
**25 g pine nuts, toasted**
**25 g sun-blushed tomatoes, drained, dried with**
  **kitchen paper and chopped**
**zest of 1 small lemon**
**4 medium skinless and boneless chicken breasts**
**25 g butter, softened**
**16 thin slices pancetta**
**salt and freshly ground black pepper**

1. Using a knife or pair of scissors carefully cut and remove the hard central stem from each cabbage leaf. Bring a large pan of water to the boil and put the cabbage leaves in the water for 1 minute. Drain and plunge into ice-cold water. When the leaves are cold, remove and dry with kitchen paper. Set aside.

2. Preheat the oven to Gas Mark 6/200°C/fan oven 180°C. In a small bowl mix together the ricotta, pine nuts, tomatoes, lemon zest and seasoning. Set aside. Place a chicken breast on a board and cut across the middle horizontally, but not right through. Open up the chicken breast, like a butterfly, and put a quarter of the ricotta filling into the centre of the chicken. Fold over the top half of the chicken to sandwich the filling. Repeat with the remaining chicken breasts and ricotta mixture.

3. Brush a large square of foil with a quarter of the butter and lay out on a clean surface. Place a cabbage leaf on the foil and then arrange four slices of pancetta across the leaf. Sit the chicken breast in the centre and carefully but tightly fold over the pancetta. Using the foil to help, firmly wrap the chicken breast in the cabbage and foil, sealing the ends. Place into a deep roasting tin, seam side up. Repeat with the remaining chicken, cabbage and pancetta to make three more parcels.

4. Add enough cold water to come a quarter of the way up the sides of the chicken parcels, then bake in the oven for 25–30 minutes until cooked. Remove from the roasting tin and set aside for 5–10 minutes. Then unroll and discard the foil. Cut each chicken breast in half diagonally and serve immediately.

# CRUNCHY PEANUT CHICKEN SALAD

You can also use roasted nuts in this salad, whichever you can find. But the smoked almonds add a wonderful South American flavour to this dish.

**serves 2**

2 skinless and boneless chicken breasts
3 tablespoons half fat crème fraîche
1 tablespoon crunchy peanut butter
2 Little Gem lettuces, shredded
1 avocado, peeled, stoned and sliced
¼ cucumber, cut into sticks
12 baby plum tomatoes, halved
50 g hickory-smoked almonds
salt and freshly ground black pepper

**for the tarragon and peanut sauce**
1 tablespoon crunchy peanut butter
juice of 1 lemon
4 tablespoons sunflower oil
3 fresh tarragon sprigs, finely chopped
½ small onion, finely grated

1. Combine all the ingredients for the sauce in a jug. Reserve 2 tablespoons in a bowl and set aside.

2. Score three cuts in each chicken breast and then put into a freezer bag. Spoon in the sauce from the jug, seal the bag and massage the chicken from the outside until the chicken is coated. Leave to marinate for 2 hours in the fridge.

3. Heat a griddle pan until hot. Remove the chicken from the freezer bag, and cook on the griddle pan for 10 minutes, turning once, until cooked. Transfer to a plate and leave to cool.

4. Meanwhile, mix the reserved marinade with the crème fraîche and peanut butter until smooth. Season with salt and black pepper. Arrange the lettuce on two plates and top with the avocado, cucumber and tomato. Cut each chicken breast into thin slices and use to top each salad. Sprinkle with the almonds and add a dollop of the crème fraîche sauce. Serve immediately.

**tip** The tarragon and peanut sauce can be used to marinate chicken, pork or beef.

# THE BLACK FARMER COQ AU VIN

Make this dish the day before and allow the flavours to really mingle. Simply reheat on the hob until piping hot. Serve with lashings of creamy mashed potato to soak up those delicious red wine juices.

**serves 4**

1.75 kg chicken, jointed into 8 pieces
300 ml full-bodied red wine
2 garlic cloves, bruised
4 fresh thyme sprigs
2 fresh bay leaves
150 ml fig balsamic vinegar
1 tablespoon olive oil
100 g pancetta, cut into thick strips
12 shallots, peeled and trimmed
1 tablespoon tomato purée
2 tablespoons plain flour
450 ml fresh chicken stock
25 g unsalted butter
150 g baby button mushrooms, trimmed
salt and freshly ground black pepper

1. Put the chicken, red wine, garlic, thyme, bay leaves and balsamic vinegar into a large freezer bag. Seal and leave to marinate for 4–8 hours in the fridge.

2. Remove the chicken from the freezer bag and reserve the marinade. Pat the chicken dry with kitchen paper and set aside. Heat the oil in a large casserole pan and cook the chicken for 5 minutes, in batches, until brown all over. Remove and set aside.

3. Add the pancetta and fry for 3–4 minutes until golden. Remove with a slotted spoon and set aside. Add the shallots and cook gently for 5 minutes until starting to brown.

4. Remove the garlic cloves from the reserved marinade and crush. Add to the casserole pan along with half the cooked pancetta. Stir in the tomato purée and flour and cook for 1 minute. Then gradually pour in the stock, stirring until combined. Pour in the reserved marinade and return the chicken pieces to the pan. Bring to the boil, cover and gently simmer for 30 minutes.

5. Remove the lid and continue to simmer for 15 minutes until the juices are slightly thickened and the chicken is cooked. Meanwhile, melt the butter in a frying pan and fry the mushrooms for 5 minutes until golden and cooked. Stir the mushrooms into the pan along with the remaining bacon. Check the seasoning and serve immediately.

' Make this dish the day before and allow the flavours to really mingle. Serve with lashings of creamy mashed potato. '

## ZESTY CHICKEN THIGHS

Stuffing the thighs with butter, thyme and lime helps to keep them incredibly succulent. Serve with new potatoes and a generous salad.

serves 4

6 spring onions, finely chopped
1 tablespoon fresh thyme leaves
2 garlic cloves, crushed
zest and juice of 2 limes
75 g butter, at room temperature
8 chicken thighs
2 tablespoons limoncello
salt and freshly ground black pepper

1. In a bowl mix together the spring onions, thyme, garlic, lime zest and butter. Season generously with salt and black pepper. Loosen the skin from one short end of each chicken thigh to make a pocket between the chicken meat and skin.
2. Spoon about 1 tablespoon of the butter mixture into the pocket. Fold under the skin and reshape the chicken thighs. Put into an ovenproof dish.
3. Pour over the lime juice and limoncello and cover with clingfilm. Leave to marinate for at least 1 hour.
4. Preheat the oven to Gas Mark 5/190°C/fan oven 170°C. Remove and discard the clingfilm from the chicken thighs. Bake in the oven for 45 minutes, basting halfway through, until the chicken is cooked and the juices run clear. Serve immediately.

## CARIBBEAN JERK CHICKEN

This classic is also great when cooked on the barbecue. Simply cook in the oven as in the recipe below for 20 minutes and then finish off for the last 10 minutes on a hot barbecue for a real chargrilled flavour. Serve with fried or baked plantain and a generous mixed salad.

serves 4

4 spring onions, roughly chopped
1 green finger chilli, roughly chopped
2 teaspoons ground allspice
½ teaspoon ground cinnamon
a pinch of ground cloves
½ teaspoon ground ginger
2 teaspoons soy sauce
juice of 3 limes
2 garlic cloves, crushed
2 tablespoons olive oil
4 chicken legs or breasts on the bone

1. Put the spring onions, green chilli, allspice, cinnamon, cloves, ginger, soy sauce, lime juice, garlic and olive oil into a small food processor and whizz to a paste. Transfer to a freezer bag and add the chicken legs.
2. Seal the bag tightly and massage the paste into the chicken until coated. Leave to marinate in the fridge for at least 2 hours or preferably overnight.
3. Preheat the oven to Gas Mark 4/180°C/fan oven 160°C. Put the chicken on a roasting tray and roast in the oven for 30 minutes or until the chicken is cooked and the juices run clear.

I have many memories of my mother spending most of her time in the kitchen, cooking. The kitchen was both her sanctuary from her herd of kids and also a domain that everyone knew was hers and hers alone, where no one was allowed except by special invitation. That invitation was usually to do all the menial tasks, but it was a pleasure to watch the master at work. My mother could spend all day in her kitchen creating wonderful dishes. As a kid I used to find it baffling why she spent so much time cooking, and it was only when I started to appreciate how she created a dish like Caribbean Jerk Chicken that I understood.

As great a cook as my mother was, she wanted me to see for myself where she had learnt her cooking skills and that meant going back to the homeland. **I remember the experience very clearly as, at nineteen, it was the first time I had been back to Jamaica for many years.**

The plane touched down after an eventful fifteen-hour flight. Getting off the plane I was hit by an unfamiliar tropical heat, sufficiently powerful to shake off the sickly, artificial aeroplane environment. So intense was the heat that it stopped me in my tracks as I made my way through my new surroundings. As my senses desperately tried to take in this unfamiliar place I was further thrown when I was greeted with the organized chaos of passport control. This is unlike any passport control I have ever encountered. Dread and apprehension now came into the mix. People were a lot more vocal and expressive than I was used to.

Having got through passport control I was greeted with a scene that sent my brain into overload. Wherever I looked I could see only black faces, which were even more expressive and vocal. Someone grabbed my suitcase and started to march off with it, at the same time speaking to me in a pidgin English that I was struggling to understand – 'wher you a go boy' were the only words that I could decipher. Not that it made any difference. Despite the tropical heat I was frozen to the spot. Now the only senses working were my vision and hearing, but even they were going into meltdown as another person started to fight the stranger who had my suitcase and tried to take it from him. The ferocity of their argument was such that I thought a murder was about to be committed over who was entitled to my luggage. If I could have manoeuvred to turn round and escape this madness I would have been on the next flight back home to England.

Just when I thought the end was nigh, charging through this mayhem was a solid 5' 6" black angel, who seemed to have the power of Moses. The sea of people parted as she purposefully marched towards her goal – the two men fighting over my suitcase. With ferocity and determination, she demanded that they 'leave de bwoy alone'. Having dealt with that situation her attention turned to me. As she approached me with arms outstretched I felt the tropical heat again, just in time to receive a hug and kiss that is given only to a long-lost loved one. **'Freddie you turn a big bwoy' is what I was able to understand.** She stroked my face as if I was a newborn baby, walking around me several times, looking me up and down and touching me all over as if trying to make sure I was not a figment of her imagination. Having convinced herself that I am real she gives me such a hug that I can hardly believe it comes from a woman in her sixties.

Secure in the fact that her loved one had arrived safely, she continued using her biblical prowess to part the human sea as she led me outside to our transportation. On the way I witnessed a lot of suitcase grabbing and verbal fighting over the luggage in question. Having regained my composure I was able to make sense of what was going on. The place was full of people touting for business. In Jamaica business is gotten by the direct approach. Competition is fierce and nothing is sacred.

My black angel eventually got me to a ramshackle bus terminal unlike any that I had seen before. Lines of old Volkswagen minibuses, brightly decorated – even these inanimate objects were in competition with each other, for from each minibus music is booming, competing for volume with its neighbours. I was shown to our minibus and what became immediately apparent was that the most treasured cargo being transported was not human, but the massive speakers that were booming the kind of music that I was used to hearing back home. My fellow passengers squeezed in between the speakers and it was only when the driver realized that if he tried to push any more passengers on we would be in danger of toppling over, that we were off.

Now the minibus driver was adding to my misgivings. Driving over potholes and swerving at breakneck speed on tight bends had me thinking I was being punished for past sins before I leave this mortal world. **Thank God for large bosoms.** I am sure they protected me from serious injury on this bus trip. As I was violently tossed around, like a car airbag they absorbed the shock every time I landed on them.

The owners of these precious pieces of equipment seem so nonchalant at my regular intrusion it is as though the driver has supplied them for this very purpose. With the aid of these mamas I arrived at my final destination, Frankfield in the parish of Clarendon, Jamaica. This is where I was born and brought up by my black angel, Miss Edna, until the age of four. 'This is the bed where you were born. This is the house where you lived. Those fields over there are where you used to help plant plantains. This is where you used to chase the pigs.' In that single moment everything started to make sense. I recognized the origin of the powerful feeling and of the dreams that I had had back home in England as a twelve-year-old boy.

After what seemed like an eternity travelling, there was a ritual that followed which made me feel wide awake. While my aunt was out meeting me, my other relatives had prepared a banquet the likes of which I had never seen before. The next dish is a recipe that I remember from that meal, the others have been influenced by the Caribbean and other exotic travel destinations, where spice and flavour is an essential for every meal.

# CAJUN BLACKENED CHICKEN THIGHS

Serve with a fresh green or tomato and onion salad with sautéed diced potatoes. Left to get cold, they make the ideal addition to any packed lunch.

serves 4

1 tablespoon smoked paprika
2 teaspoons mild chilli powder
1 teaspoon onion granules
1 teaspoon garlic granules
1 teaspoon dried sage
1 teaspoon dried oregano
1 teaspoon dried thyme
½ teaspoon ground black pepper
2 teaspoons cornflour
2 teaspoons light muscovado sugar
8 chicken thighs

1. Put the paprika, chilli powder, onion and garlic granules, sage, oregano, thyme, pepper, cornflour and sugar into a freezer bag. Seal the bag and shake to mix.
2. Add the chicken thighs to the freezer bag, seal again and massage the chicken thighs to coat in the spices. Leave to marinate for at least 1 hour or up to 12 hours in the fridge.
3. Preheat the oven to Gas Mark 6/200°C/fan oven 190°C, or heat the barbecue. Cook the chicken thighs in the oven or on the barbecue for 20–25 minutes, until cooked and the juices run clear. Leave to rest for 5 minutes, then serve.

# SPICY CHICKEN JAMBALAYA

This dish is often attributed to the cooking of New Orleans.

serves 4–6

2 tablespoons olive oil
450 g skinless and boneless chicken thighs, cut into chunks
2 streaky bacon rashers, chopped
150 g chorizo with chilli, cut into small chunks
1 onion, chopped
1 garlic clove, crushed
1 scotch bonnet chilli, finely sliced
1 red pepper, deseeded and diced
1 green pepper, deseeded and diced
200 g long grain white rice
½ teaspoon ground ginger
1 tablespoon tomato purée
450 ml chicken stock
150 g peeled cooked prawns
a small handful of fresh coriander
salt and freshly ground black pepper

1. Heat the oil in a lidded wide pan and cook the chicken chunks for 5 minutes, turning until brown all over. Remove and set aside. Add the bacon and fry for 2 minutes until cooked and crispy. Remove and set aside. Put the chorizo into the pan and cook for 2–3 minutes until starting to char. Remove with a slotted spoon and drain on kitchen paper.
2. Add the onion, garlic, chilli and peppers to the pan and gently cook for 5–8 minutes until starting to soften and brown. Stir in the rice and ginger until coated in the oil. Then stir in the tomato purée and cook for 30 seconds. Gradually pour in the chicken stock, stirring until combined, then return the browned chicken and bacon to the pan. Bring to the boil, then cover and simmer for 10 minutes.
3. Remove the lid and stir in the chorizo and prawns. Replace the lid and cook for a further 5 minutes until the rice is tender, the chicken is cooked and there is barely any liquid left. Check the seasoning. Serve sprinkled with coriander.

## SPICY CHICKEN FAJITAS

Serve wrapped in flour tortillas with grated cheese, sour cream, diced tomatoes and guacamole.

serves 4

4 skinless and boneless chicken breasts
1 tablespoon olive oil
1 large onion, thinly sliced
3 mixed peppers, deseeded and thinly sliced
8 flour tortillas

for the mixed herb and chilli paste
2 teaspoons ground ginger
1 teaspoon hot paprika
50 ml olive oil
2 teaspoons garlic purée
1 tablespoon dried flat-leaf parsley
1–1½ tablespoons harissa paste (depending on how hot you like it)
2 tablespoons finely chopped fresh coriander
2 tablespoons white wine vinegar
salt and freshly ground black pepper

1. In a bowl mix together all the ingredients for the mixed herb and chilli paste. Season generously. Score each chicken breast about three times and put into a freezer bag. Spoon in the chilli paste and seal the bag. Massage the chicken from the outside so that it is coated in the paste. Leave to marinate for at least 1 hour or overnight in the fridge.
2. When ready to cook, preheat the grill or barbecue to medium. Cook the chicken breasts for 5–6 minutes on each side or until cooked and the juices run clear. Put on a board and loosely cover with foil.
3. Meanwhile, heat the oil in a wide frying pan and cook the onion and peppers for 5–8 minutes until softened and starting to brown. Warm the tortilla wraps according to pack instructions. To serve, slice the chicken into thin strips and toss through the onions and peppers. Serve immediately in the warmed tortilla wraps.

## ROAST CHICKEN PAD THAI

East meets West with this classic dish from Thailand. Leftover roast chicken works really well, but you could use diced raw chicken. Simply pan fry in a little oil first, then add instead of the cooked chicken.

serves 2

150 g medium rice noodles
2 tablespoons tamarind paste
2 tablespoons caster sugar
3 teaspoons fish sauce
½ teaspoon dried chilli flakes
juice of 1 lime plus wedges to serve
2 tablespoons groundnut oil
1 banana shallot, finely chopped
3 garlic cloves, crushed
200 g cooked roast chicken, shredded
3 spring onions, sliced
1 egg
60 g bean sprouts
25 g roasted peanuts, chopped

1. Soak the noodles in boiling water for 5–6 minutes or according to pack instructions, until tender and flexible but not overly swollen. Meanwhile, in a bowl mix together the tamarind paste, sugar, fish sauce, chilli flakes and lime juice. Drain the noodles and set both aside.
2. Heat the oil in a large wok until hot and stir fry the shallot and garlic for 1–2 minutes. Add the drained noodles, shredded chicken and spring onions and pour in the tamarind mix, stirring continuously for 1–2 minutes until combined.
3. Push the noodles to one side of the wok and break an egg into the pan. Let the egg start to set for about 1 minute, then stir to break up like scrambled egg and mix into the noodles. Continue to stir fry for 2–3 minutes until everything is combined. Divide between two plates. Top each serving with half the bean sprouts and sprinkle over the peanuts. Serve immediately with lime wedges.

This last chicken dish I will dedicate to my daughter Scarlett, as it is a dish that we often make together. All the women in my family seem to have certain things in common. They are strong, determined and have a sense of responsibility for the people around them, be they family, friend or stranger. My mother and aunt Miss Edna would go without themselves to make sure that everyone else around is fed and watered. These women seem to be permanently fixing other people's problems. They were the ones who wore the trousers in the household. They were the sort of people who I knew would fight tooth and nail for their kinfolk.

In the debate on what makes us the people we are – nature or nurture – I come down firmly on the side of nature. In my daughter I can see these great women's natures running through her very being. Scarlett is only ten and already she has this sense of wider responsibility, the need to look after others, a grit and wisdom much more developed than her age. A gift passed down through her DNA, which will see her through life's ups and downs.

All these women and Scarlett are at their best when they are cooking for a group of people. This is their opportunity to show off their natural tendency to make people feel good and, more importantly, show off their creativity. The kitchen is their canvas and the ingredients their paint. They cook with passion and completing a dish gives them a sense of achievement.

We have such little time with our children and soon all that I will have left are memories, when Scarlett eventually flies the nest and makes her own way in the world. For me, cooking this next dish with Scarlett will be another of my most precious memories – reminding me of the beauty of seeing a personality emerging.

# SCARLETT'S CHICKEN AND POTATO BAKE

This is simply divine – creamy dauphinoise-like potatoes topped with succulent chicken and a golden cheesy crust. Serve with cooked green beans, asparagus and peas.

**serves 4**

350 g floury potatoes, thinly sliced

2 tablespoons olive oil

500 g skinless and boneless chicken thighs

1 onion, sliced

2 garlic cloves, crushed

3 Black Farmer Hickory Smoked Bacon rashers, chopped

150 ml dry white wine

150 ml double cream

50 g grated mature Cheddar or Gruyère cheese

1 tablespoon snipped fresh chives

salt and freshly ground black pepper

1. Preheat the oven to Gas Mark 6/200°C/fan oven 180°C. Put the potato slices into a pan of cold salted water and bring to the boil. Simmer for 2 minutes then carefully drain. Leave to completely drain in a colander.

2. Meanwhile, heat half the oil in a frying pan and cook the chicken thighs for 5 minutes, turning until brown. You will have to do this in batches. Remove and set aside. Add the remaining oil to the pan and gently cook the onion and garlic for 3–4 minutes, until starting to soften. Add the bacon and continue to cook for a further 3 minutes until the bacon is starting to brown and go crispy.

3. Remove the onion, garlic and bacon from the pan with a slotted spoon and set aside. Return the pan to the heat and add the white wine. Allow to bubble for 1 minute to deglaze the pan, then add the cream and take off the heat. Season generously.

4. Arrange the potato slices in the bottom of an ovenproof dish, overlapping the edges slightly. Put the chicken thighs over the top to cover the potatoes and then arrange the onion and bacon mixture over the chicken. Pour over the cream and wine mixture and sprinkle the cheese over the top.

5. Cover with foil and bake in the oven for 30 minutes. Remove the foil and cook for a further 30 minutes until golden and bubbling and the potatoes are tender. Sprinkle with the chives and serve immediately.

But after all that chicken, I cannot forget to share my love for duck. I was first introduced to duck many years ago via a Chinese takeaway – not glamorous I know. I ordered Peking duck with a plum sauce not knowing particularly what to expect, but once I had figured out how to put the dish together I was smitten. Now, whenever I eat Chinese, Peking duck is always top of my list. I often watch my children as we eat and see the same excitement I must have had when I first tried the dish. I love the ritual of shredding the duck off the bone and placing it onto the delicate pancake, combining it with cucumber sticks and plum sauce. The combination of flavours and textures is brilliant. The next recipe is my version of this great classic.

For many years the only times I enjoyed the pleasure of duck were when I ordered a Chinese. Although I really loved the taste I was unsure how to cook the bird, which I understood to be rather fatty with not a lot of meat. However, when I started to look around for new products to introduce under The Black Farmer brand, I happened upon a West Country family firm called Creedy Carver who raise free-range birds in the time-honoured fashion, to encourage the slow natural growth that gives the birds real flavour. My main object was to talk to them about their chicken, but during a visit they gave me some duck and goose to take home and try. With my trusty Good Housekeeping cookbook to hand (always a good reference book for basics), I roasted my first duck. Yes it was fattier than chicken and with not as much meat, but it was truly flavoursome and incredibly tender. With ever-growing confidence, I developed a few recipes to show just how versatile duck can be.

# CRISPY ROAST DUCK

### with Mango and Chilli Sauce

Let everyone get stuck in and serve with steamed Chinese pancakes, shredded spring onion and cucumber for a real finger food treat.

serves 4

1.8 kg whole duck

for the mango and chilli sauce
1 tablespoon olive oil
1 onion, finely chopped
1 red chilli, sliced
25 g fresh ginger, peeled and grated
2 ripe mangoes, peeled, stoned and cubed
50 ml white wine vinegar
2 tablespoons caster sugar
300 ml chicken stock
salt and freshly ground black pepper

1. Remove the packaging from the duck and pat dry with kitchen paper. Put on a plate and chill in the fridge for 24 hours.
2. The next day, heat the oil in a saucepan and cook the onion for 3–4 minutes until softened. Add the chilli, ginger and mangoes and cook for a further 3–4 minutes. Add the vinegar, sugar and stock and bring to the boil. Simmer gently for 30 minutes until the liquid has evaporated.
3. Transfer half to a jug and whizz with a hand blender until smooth. Stir back into the saucepan with the unblended mango. Season and set aside to cool.
4. Preheat the oven to Gas Mark 7/220°C/fan oven 200°C. Prick the duck all over with a skewer and then place on a wire rack inside a large roasting tin. Roast in the middle of the oven for 1 hour 50 minutes, carefully draining the fat from the roasting tin two or three times during cooking.
5. Remove the duck from the oven and loosely cover with foil. Leave to rest for 20 minutes, then carve or shred and serve with the mango and chilli sauce.

# SWEET AND SOUR ELDERFLOWER DUCK

There is something about the richness of duck that goes so well with fruit. The sour gooseberries and the sweet elderflower make an amazing combination. You can use fresh or frozen gooseberries, whichever you have available.

serves 2

200 ml white wine
150 g gooseberries, topped and tailed
2 duck breasts with skin on
1 onion, sliced
125 ml elderflower cordial
100 ml chicken stock
salt and freshly ground black pepper

1. Put the white wine into a small pan and bring to the boil. Bubble rapidly for 1–2 minutes, then add the gooseberries. Lower the heat and poach gently for 5 minutes until just soft. Transfer to a jug and whizz with a hand blender until smooth. Pass through a sieve into a clean bowl. Set aside.
2. Heat a non-stick frying pan until hot. Cook the duck breasts skin side down for 5 minutes to start rendering the fat. Reduce the heat and gently cook for a further 10–15 minutes, turning, until the duck is cooked and the skin is golden brown and crispy. Remove the duck breasts and loosely wrap in foil. Set aside.
3. Discard the fat from the frying pan apart from about 1 tablespoon. Return the pan to the heat and gently cook the onion for 3–4 minutes until starting to soften. Add the cordial and rapidly bubble for 2–3 minutes until reduced.
4. Pour in the gooseberry purée and chicken stock and bubble for a further 2–3 minutes until reduced by half. Season well. To serve, cut the duck into slices on the diagonal and serve with the sauce.

# SWEET GINGER DUCK NOODLE STIR FRY

The great thing about stir fries is that you can really add whichever vegetables you like or, if you want to save time, use a ready-prepared bag of stir fry vegetables. The only secret to a good stir fry is to ensure you have all your ingredients chopped and prepared ready to go.

serves 2

2 duck breasts with skin on
100 g dried medium egg noodles
1 tablespoon groundnut oil
1 onion, chopped
2 garlic cloves, sliced
50 g fresh ginger, peeled and shredded
½ red pepper, deseeded and sliced
100 g baby corn, halved
100 g mange tout, halved diagonally
100 g pak choi, leaves and stalks separated

for the sweet ginger sauce
125 g runny honey
juice of 2 lemons
1 teaspoon ground ginger
¼ teaspoon ground turmeric

1. In a bowl mix together all the ingredients for the sweet ginger sauce. Put the duck breasts into a shallow non-metallic dish and pour over the sauce. Turn to coat in the marinade and then set aside for up to 1 hour.

2. Remove the duck from the marinade, wipe off excess marinade with your hands and pat dry with kitchen paper. Reserve the marinade. Heat a non-stick frying pan until hot. Cook the duck breasts skin side down for 5 minutes to start rendering the fat. Reduce the heat and gently cook for a further 10–15 minutes, turning, until the duck is cooked and the skin is golden brown and crispy. Remove the duck breasts and loosely wrap in foil. Set aside.

3. Meanwhile, cook the noodles according to pack instructions until tender. Drain and set aside.

4. Heat a wok until really hot and add the oil. Stir fry the onion for 3 minutes, stirring constantly, and then add the garlic and ginger and fry for a further 1 minute until softened and starting to brown.

5. Add the pepper and baby corn and stir fry for a further 3 minutes. Then stir in the mange tout and pak choi stalks and cook for 3–5 minutes, stirring occasionally, until just tender.

6. Pour in the reserved marinade, pak choi leaves and cooked noodles and bubble for 1–2 minutes, stirring to combine and coat the noodles in sauce. Slice the duck breasts on the diagonal and serve in bowls on top of the noodles.

tip The sweet ginger sauce also works really well with chicken and fish.

# THAI DUCK CURRY

Don't be put off by the cooking time of this curry. Patience is everything as the legs of this bird need slow cooking.

**serves 4**

6 duck legs
900 ml chicken stock
2 g dried sliced Thai galangal or 15 g fresh galangal, peeled and sliced
1 red chilli, halved
1 tablespoon groundnut oil
1 red onion, finely chopped
3 garlic cloves, finely chopped
250 g mooli, peeled and diced
4 freeze-dried lime leaves
1 tablespoon caster sugar
2–3 tablespoons red Thai curry paste
400 ml can coconut milk
Thai fish sauce for seasoning
shredded spring onions, fresh coriander leaves and lime wedges to serve

1. Heat a large lidded non-stick pan and cook the duck legs for 5 minutes until browned all over. You may need to do this in batches. Drain away the fat. Return the pan to the heat and add the chicken stock, galangal and chilli to the duck legs. Bring to the boil, cover and gently simmer for 1–1½ hours until the duck meat falls off the bone.

2. Meanwhile, heat the oil in a wide pan and cook the onion, garlic and mooli for 10 minutes until starting to soften. Add the lime leaves, sugar and curry paste and cook for 1 minute. Pour in the coconut milk and bring to the boil. Remove from the heat and set aside.

3. With a slotted spoon remove the duck legs from the pan and transfer to a plate. Leave to cool. Meanwhile, with a ladle, reserve 300 ml of the duck cooking liquid and set aside in a jug. When the duck is cool enough, remove and discard the skin. Shred the meat into bite-size pieces and set aside. Discard the bones.

4. Carefully discard the fat from the reserved cooking liquid and add the liquid to the coconut milk mixture along with the shredded duck meat. Bring to a simmer and cook for 10 minutes. Check seasoning and add fish sauce to taste. Serve immediately, topped with spring onions and coriander with lime wedges on the side.

' Thai galangal is from the ginger family and is used in a lot of Thai cooking, but if you can't find it dried or fresh then replace it with normal fresh root ginger. '

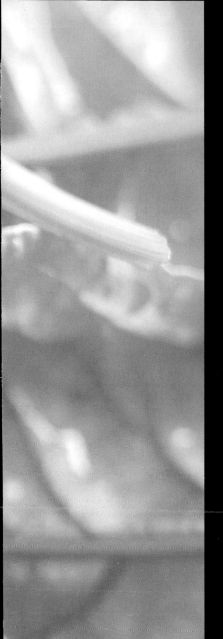

# VEGETABLES

To my surprise it was still standing there. It had been battered for decades by the weather, with only a smattering of the original blue paint that had once adorned this sad-looking structure remaining. A big hole was all that was left where once there was a window, far too elegant for its surroundings. The door had come off long ago. Lying on the ground, it had become the home for colonies of insects. The black asphalt that covered the roof had become green, layered with moss and weeds as Mother Nature relentlessly tried to bring this building under her control and get it to blend into her environment.

This simple six-foot-square wooden garden shed had been there for forty years and, although it was on its last legs, it seemed as though it was hanging on for my visit before it would give in to the elements and collapse. And with that collapse would go the memories that it had held for me since I was a boy. When I visited our old allotment with an Australian film crew in the spring of 2006 I didn't expect the shed to be clinging on, and seeing it took me back to those days. It was in this very shed that I made myself a promise that would steer me through my life.

When I was ten I built this shed with my dad. At the time I felt that my father was constructing it with an intensity of love, care and attention that was uncharacteristic of the man. This was his pride and joy and he

was building a shed that would last. Little did I know at the time, but building this shed was to be something that would set me on a course that would affect the rest of my life. My father died some twenty years ago and I am sure he would have been proud to see that regardless of what nature had thrown at it, this shed had managed to stand up to the elements for forty years and shouted to all that 'I will not be beaten'. This shed took pride of place in our allotment, which, along with my father, I was responsible for maintaining. This allotment became my oasis from the misery of inner-city living. While I was at the allotment I could forget all my troubles and woes and focus my attention on nurturing the vegetables we grew on this plot. On cold and wet days the shed was a welcome sanctuary, on hot days it provided much needed shade. As well as providing shelter this shed also housed the tools of our labour and it became my classroom, where my father taught me how to plant the vegetables that would end up on our dinner plates.

Vegetables are all too often forgotten when it comes to recipes; the focus of the meal tending to be on the meats. Now I am an unreconstructed carnivore and I love my meat, but growing vegetables played such an important part in my life I thought it only right to include some of my favourites here. These can either act as a great accompaniment to other dishes in this book or, for the vegetarians out there, some could be a meal in themselves.

## CORIANDER ROASTED CARROTS

The excitement you get from pulling your first carrot is carried through to the enjoyment you will get from eating this dish. Roasting the carrots brings out their natural sugars, which marry with the Sichuan pepper and coriander seeds. You'll never boil a carrot again!

**serves 4**

500 g carrots, scrubbed and trimmed

1 teaspoon Sichuan pepper

2 teaspoons coriander seeds

2 tablespoons olive oil

a few fresh thyme sprigs

2 garlic cloves, sliced

2 tablespoons maple syrup

25 g butter, cut into cubes

salt

1. Preheat the oven to Gas Mark 6/200°C/fan oven 180°C. Cut the carrots in half lengthways and then in half again. Put into a large non-stick roasting tin.

2. Put the Sichuan pepper and coriander seeds into a mortar and pestle and lightly crush. Drizzle the carrots with the olive oil and sprinkle over the crushed pepper and seeds, thyme and garlic. Lightly toss to coat and then roast in the oven for 30 minutes, turning the carrots halfway through.

3. Remove the carrots from the oven and drizzle with maple syrup and dot over the butter. Roast in the oven for a further 10–15 minutes until starting to caramelize. Season with salt and serve immediately.

## SPICED ROAST POTATOES

Roasties don't get better than this! Golden crunchiness on the outside and creamy in the middle – the perfect way to jazz up a Sunday roast.

**serves 4**

900 g floury potatoes such as King Edward or Desirée, peeled and cut into even chunks

½ teaspoon turmeric

1 tablespoon smoked paprika

2 teaspoons ground cumin

1 tablespoon plain flour

2 tablespoons goose fat

salt

1. Preheat the oven to Gas Mark 6/200°C/fan oven 180°C. Put the potatoes into a pan of cold salted water and bring to the boil. Simmer for 5–8 minutes until the edges start to soften. Meanwhile, mix together the turmeric, paprika, cumin and flour. Set aside. Drain the potatoes thoroughly and return to the pan.

2. Put the goose fat into a roasting tin and put into the oven. Return the pan with the potatoes to a gentle heat and cook for 30 seconds, shaking the pan to evaporate any excess moisture. Remove from the heat and add the spiced flour. Cover with a lid and carefully shake the pan until the potatoes are coated in the spiced flour and the edges of the potatoes are fluffed up.

3. Remove the roasting tin from the oven and add the potatoes. Turn to coat in the hot fat and roast in the oven for 1 hour until golden and crispy. Season with salt and serve immediately.

With eleven of us living in that small terraced house space was very restricted, and for as long as I could remember I had to share a double bed with two of my brothers. My overriding memory of the family home is of the lack of space. During the day it was fine – I could escape to the allotment – but at night eleven bodies had to be crammed into every available corner in order to find a bit of personal space.

For my own sanity I knew I would have to move out as soon as I could. Being a failure at school I didn't have much choice in how I was going to escape my family prison, but escape I must. With the foolishness of youth, hungry to have my own space and desperate to have my own bed, at sixteen I decided I would join the army. I got my own bed all right, but it never crossed my mind that I would be sharing a dormitory with twelve other teenagers.

Army discipline was a shock to my system. The NCOs were not like the teachers at my secondary modern who would put up with all kinds of abuse from the pupils. For several tortuous months the army tried to lick me into shape and get me to act like a team player. The experience was hell. In those days you were not going to be doing yourself any favours if you were a cocky, loud-mouthed pain in the arse. And if you added being black to that mix...

Well, that was the final straw, and it got some of my NCOs to the point of such extreme rage that more often than not I ended up getting some sort of kicking. These kickings were intended to let me know my rightful station in life: i.e. on the rubbish heap.

Yet, as hard as the beatings may have been, it was better than being at home. Looking back, I don't know why I didn't just knuckle down and keep my mouth shut. It was not a happy time for me and when I used to go to the mess for meals I would chastise myself for not joining the catering division rather than the infantry. Surely cooking had to be much better than the punishment I was taking?

I eventually got kicked out of the army and, quite frankly, they were glad to see the back of me. I hold no grudges because, as tough as it was, it was the start of getting me out of my prison at home. My next idea was to try my hand at cooking and I enrolled in a catering course, after which followed a series of jobs...

Three of us worked in the kitchen of what I regarded as the trendiest restaurant in Birmingham. After weeks of waiting, a new machine was delivered. Our angst had built to fever pitch by the time it was installed and we feared that this new equipment would do us serious harm. One of us had to take the plunge.

Ours was the only restaurant in Birmingham at that time to have a charcoal gas grill. It had been specially shipped over from the States to cook the burgers for which our establishment was famous. This grill was in all the marketing material and was a great selling point. So why did we need this other monstrous machine, which reputedly could cause the user serious harm, even death?

Fresh food at this particular restaurant was a big no-no. Everything was frozen. This was the age when frozen food ruled our eating habits in and out of the home. And frozen's great friend 'canned', be it sweetcorn, tomatoes or vegetables, was what many restaurants used as a matter of course in those dark days. We called ourselves chefs but quite frankly monkeys could have done just as well.

My boss at the time, an ex-accountant by the way, was always looking for new ways to save money. He was a frozen and canned food evangelist. And it was this evangelism that had taken him to the point of putting our lives in danger. This was a man who had no passion for food – he just loved seeing how he could cut costs. When I eventually got the opportunity to work in French and Italian restaurants, not only were my eyes opened to what it means to be passionate about food but I discovered that, in these environments, using frozen food was a sackable offence, whereas at the hamburger joint it was wastage that was the sackable offence. To this end Mr Frozen had come up with the perfect time-saving device: I would argue that I was one of the first in this country to use a microwave oven. The microwave was used to defrost the burgers and added to the overall unpleasantness of the cooking.

Microwaves are now a fundamental part of every kitchen and, used properly, they can be an excellent cooking aid. Back then, the word was that these machines could cook your insides, so in an effort to protect ourselves against such an eventuality, the most junior person in the kitchen had to do all the microwave cooking. Even to this day I keep my microwave use down to a minimum, not through any fear of my insides being cooked but because I don't feel food tastes as good when cooked this way.

# SPICED RUNNER BEANS

You will find pickling spices in the herb and spice section in the supermarket.

serves 2–4

250 g runner beans, topped and tailed
1 tablespoon olive oil
½ red onion, finely sliced
1 tablespoon caster sugar
½ tablespoon pickling spices, crushed
juice of ½ lemon
salt and freshly ground black pepper

1. Using a bean cutter, slice the runner beans into spaghetti-like strands, discarding the stringy sides. If you don't have a bean cutter, use a potato peeler to remove the stringy side bits and then cut the beans into short lengths or long strands.
2. Bring a large pan of salted water to the boil and cook the runner beans for 3–4 minutes until they are tender but still have a bite. Drain and set aside in a colander.
3. Heat the oil in a large wide saucepan and cook the onion and sugar slowly for 5–8 minutes until softened and starting to caramelize. Add the pickling spices and continue to cook for a further 5 minutes, stirring occasionally.
4. Add the cooked runner beans and toss to coat in the onion mixture. Cook gently until the beans are coated and heated through. Season with salt and black pepper, squeeze over the lemon juice and serve immediately.

# MUSHY PEAS

Adding a touch of hot pepper sauce gives a real powerful kick. Add as much or as little as you like. These go really well with Crispy Fish and Chips (page 160).

serves 4–6

400 g garden peas, fresh or frozen
45 g butter
1 vegetable stock cube
½ teaspoon dried mint
25 g Parmesan cheese, grated
1–2 tablespoons hot pepper sauce, to taste
salt and freshly ground black pepper

1. Defrost frozen peas or blanch fresh peas in boiling water for 3 minutes then drain. Reserve a quarter of the peas in a bowl and set aside.
2. Melt the butter in a wide frying pan and add the stock cube and 50 ml cold water. Add the remaining peas and dried mint and simmer gently for 3–4 minutes.
3. Transfer the peas and any pan juices to a blender, or use a stick blender, and purée until smooth. Transfer to a clean saucepan and stir in the reserved peas and the Parmesan. Stir in the hot pepper sauce to taste and season with salt and black pepper. Gently reheat if necessary and then serve.

# WARM GREEN BEAN SALAD
### with Slow-Roasted Chilli Tomatoes

This dish takes a little bit of patience, but once the tomatoes are in the oven you can kick back and relax. Why not make a large batch of the tomatoes? They can be stored in olive oil in the fridge for up to a month.

serves 4

450 g green beans, topped but not tailed, and halved
2 shallots, finely chopped
4 tablespoons extra virgin olive oil
2 tablespoons white balsamic vinegar
1 teaspoon Dijon mustard
a small handful of chopped mixed fresh herbs,
    such as parsley, chives and chervil
salt and freshly ground black pepper

for the slow-roasted chilli tomatoes
12 small vine tomatoes, halved
1 teaspoon caster sugar
a generous pinch of dried chilli flakes
½ teaspoon salt

1. Preheat the oven to Gas Mark 1/140°C/fan oven 120°C. Put the tomatoes on a non-stick baking tray, cut side up and well spaced apart. Sprinkle the sugar, chilli flakes and salt over the cut side of the tomatoes. Cook slowly in the oven for 3 hours until the tomatoes are wrinkly and shrivelled.
2. When the tomatoes are cooked, remove from the oven and set aside. Bring a pan of salted water to the boil and cook the green beans for 5 minutes until just cooked.
3. Meanwhile, in a large salad bowl whisk together the shallots, olive oil, vinegar and mustard. Season with salt and black pepper.
4. Drain the green beans thoroughly and then empty into the salad bowl. Toss to coat in the dressing. Add the roasted tomatoes and herbs and gently toss to combine. Leave to stand for 5 minutes before serving.

# SUMMER TOMATO SALAD

Come the summer months there is nothing better than the aroma that wafts from greenhouses or conservatories that are bursting with home-grown tomato plants, which is why this salad is a must. Never store your tomatoes in the fridge as the texture and flavour will rapidly change to something totally different from the true fruit. Choose whichever tomatoes you like for this salad, be it beef tomatoes, cherry tomatoes, yellow or green tomatoes – the choice is yours.

serves 4–6

750 g mixed tomatoes
75 ml extra virgin olive oil
30 ml red wine vinegar
30 g marinated fresh anchovy fillets, finely chopped
1 garlic clove, chopped
1 teaspoon coriander seeds, crushed
2 spring onions, finely chopped
a pinch of caster sugar
1 tablespoon chopped fresh flat-leaf parsley
2 tablespoons fresh Greek basil leaves
salt and freshly ground black pepper

1. Cut the tomatoes in halves or quarters depending on size and put into a large salad bowl.
2. In a jug mix together the oil, vinegar, anchovies, garlic, coriander seeds, spring onions and sugar. Season generously.
3. Drizzle the dressing over the tomatoes and toss to coat thoroughly. Fold through the parsley and basil and leave to infuse for at least 15 minutes before serving.

## THAI-STYLE BROAD BEANS

If you have time on your hands and your broad beans are on the older side of life, then it is quite easy to remove them from their skins for a better taste.

serves 4

2 tablespoons extra virgin olive oil
1 tablespoon cider vinegar
juice of 2 limes
1 tablespoon toasted sesame oil
1 tablespoon Thai chilli sauce
1 teaspoon Thai fish sauce
½ red onion, finely chopped
1 fresh lemongrass stick, outer leaves removed
    and stalk finely chopped
350 g fresh or frozen broad beans
2 tablespoons chopped fresh coriander
freshly ground black pepper

1. Bring a large pan of salted water to the boil. Meanwhile, mix together the olive oil, vinegar, lime juice, sesame oil, chilli sauce, fish sauce, onion and lemongrass in a jug. Season with black pepper.

2. Add the broad beans to the boiling water and cook for 3 minutes until tender. Drain thoroughly and return to the pan. Add the dressing and toss to coat. Check seasoning, adding a little more fish sauce if necessary and black pepper. Fold through the coriander and spoon into a serving dish. Leave to infuse for 5 minutes before serving.

## THREE-MUSTARD CAULIFLOWER CHEESE

This is the ultimate in comfort food. I find it hard to resist eating the whole dish before I have summoned the family for dinner.

serves 4

1 large cauliflower, cut into florets
1 leek, sliced
50 g butter
25 g plain flour
500 ml creamy Jersey milk
75 g mature Gruyère cheese, grated
1 teaspoon Dijon mustard
1 teaspoon whole grain mustard
1 teaspoon mustard powder
30 g mature Cheddar cheese, grated
salt and freshly ground black pepper

1. Preheat the oven to Gas Mark 4/180°C/fan oven 160°C. Bring a large pan of cold salted water to the boil. Plunge in the cauliflower florets and cook for 5 minutes. Then add the leek and cook for 2 minutes. Drain in a colander and set aside to drain thoroughly.

2. Meanwhile, melt the butter in another large saucepan and add the flour. Cook for 1 minute until frothy and glossy. Remove from the heat and gradually whisk in the milk until smooth and combined. Return to the heat and gently bring to the boil, stirring constantly. Cook for 1 minute until thickened. Remove from the heat and stir in the Gruyère, Dijon and whole grain mustards and the mustard powder. Season generously.

3. Add the blanched cauliflower and leek to the cheese sauce and stir to coat. Empty into a large ovenproof dish, using a spoon to even out and level the cauliflower. Sprinkle with the Cheddar cheese and bake in the oven for 45 minutes until golden and bubbling. Serve immediately.

# 7-SPICED SAVOY CABBAGE

The stench of cabbage being stewed to within an inch of its life is enough to put anyone off. This is a great way to serve up such a wonderful green. You can use any type of greens from curly kale to spring greens.

**serves 4**

1 savoy cabbage, outer leaves removed, cored and
    finely shredded
2 tablespoons groundnut oil
1 red onion, thinly sliced
a piece of pared lemon rind
30 g butter

**for the 7-spice mix**
¼ teaspoon paprika
¼ teaspoon ground mace
a pinch of ground cinnamon
½ teaspoon dried oregano
½ teaspoon cumin seeds
¼ teaspoon ground coriander
¼ teaspoon tropical peppercorns

1. Put all the ingredients for the 7-spice mix into a mortar and pestle. Crush until combined. Set aside.
2. Bring a large pan of salted water to the boil. Plunge in the cabbage and cook for 2 minutes. Drain in a colander and squeeze out as much water as possible, using a potato masher.
3. Heat the oil in a large wok and stir fry the onion for 1–2 minutes. Add the spice mix and lemon rind and cook for 30 seconds. Add the blanched cabbage and stir fry for a further 2–3 minutes, stirring continuously until combined and the cabbage is tender. Remove from the heat and fold through the butter until melted. Serve immediately.

# PANCETTA BRUSSELS SPROUTS

This is a great way to jazz up your sprouts at Christmas, but don't just save them for Christmas Day – enjoy them throughout the winter months.

**serves 4**

450 g Brussels sprouts, trimmed
25 g pine nuts
100 g diced pancetta
2 garlic cloves, crushed
50 ml dry white wine
200 ml crème fraîche
salt and freshly ground black pepper

1. Bring a pan of salted water to the boil. Add the Brussels sprouts and bring back to the boil. Simmer for 7–8 minutes until just tender. Drain and set aside.
2. Heat a large frying pan and toast the pine nuts for a few minutes until golden. Remove and set aside. Add the pancetta to the pan and cook for 5 minutes until starting to go crispy.
3. Add the Brussels sprouts and garlic and gently fry for 3 minutes. Pour in the wine and bubble rapidly until well reduced. Stir in the crème fraîche together with the pine nuts and gently bring to a simmer. Bubble until thickened, season with freshly ground black pepper and serve immediately.

# BEETROOT AND COCONUT RELISH

This is the perfect way to use up an abundance of beetroot. But remember to wear rubber gloves when peeling the beetroot otherwise you will end up with pink hands! It will last for up to a year when stored in a cool dry place in sterilized jars.

**makes 750 g**

500 g raw beetroot, trimmed, peeled and diced
350 g cooking apples, peeled, cored and chopped
1 large onion, finely chopped
300 ml cider vinegar
175 g caster sugar
1 tablespoon ground ginger
50 g unsweetened desiccated coconut
salt and freshly ground black pepper

1. Put the beetroot, apple, onion, vinegar, sugar, ginger and 200 ml water into a large pan. Gently heat, stirring occasionally, until the sugar has dissolved.

2. Bring to a simmer and gently bubble uncovered for about 1 hour, stirring occasionally, until no excess liquid remains, the mixture is thick and pulpy and the beetroot is tender.

3. Stir in the coconut and season generously. Spoon the chutney into sterilized jars (see tip), seal with vinegar-proof lids and label.

**tip** It is best to sterilize the bottles and jars in advance so they're ready and waiting to be filled. Thoroughly wash new and used jars in hot soapy water. Then either put the upturned jars on a baking sheet and heat in a preheated oven, Gas Mark 1/140°C/fan oven 120°C, for 10–15 minutes, or run the upturned jars through a hot dishwasher cycle.

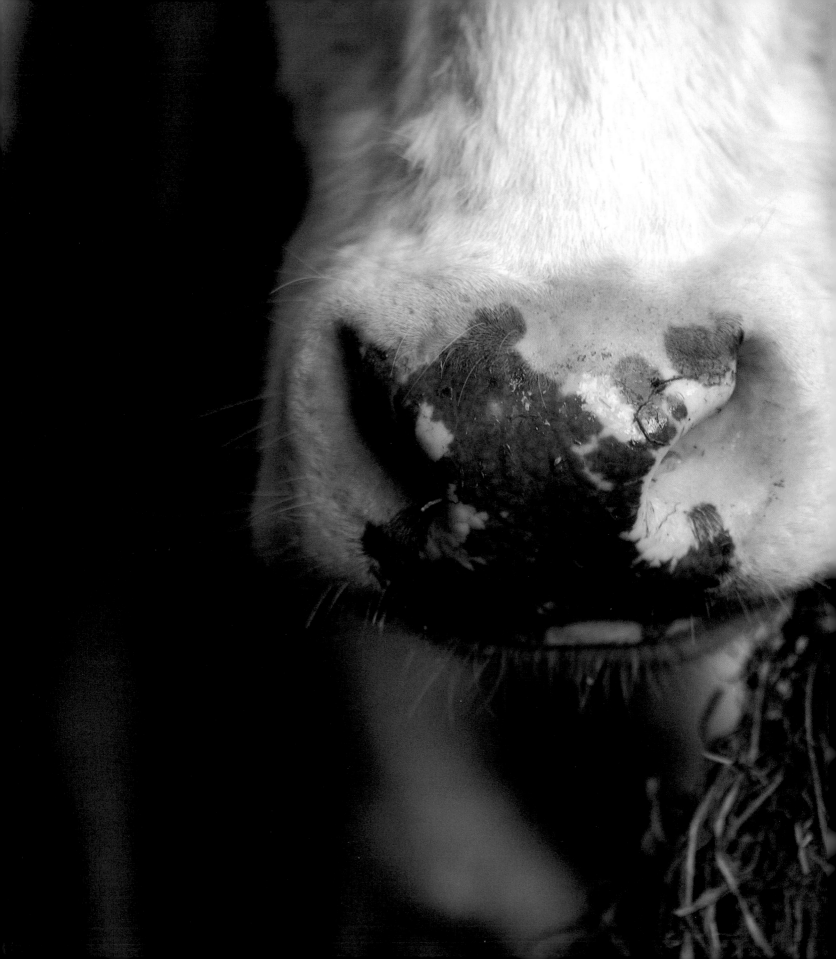

# BEEF

It was pouring with rain and the traffic was awful. It was one of those miserable late afternoons in December when it starts to get dark at 4 p.m. To further deepen my miserable mood I found myself in the centre of the West End of London trying to get to my London home. Caught in the middle of this rainstorm, my only shelter was my car. Dodging my way through traffic and crowds of people also trying to seek shelter, reaching my car became my sole purpose. By the time I got to my car I was half drenched.

With the car heater turned up to maximum, the chill of the rain was soon driven out. As Radio Four played in the background it was like having a comforting friend handing me a towel to help me dry out and soothe my chilled bones. My car had proved once again that it is a wonderful sanctuary from such bad weather. Having dried out and relaxed enough to think about the evening ahead, I discovered that the rain hadn't quite finished with me yet. The bad weather now wanted to challenge everything that I believed in.

I was due to cook dinner that evening and I wanted to make a wonderful beef dish. Something that would both fill us up and warm us against the awful winter weather. Beef is a wonderful winter food, a good comfort food. During the early part of the day I was toying between making one of the two following dishes. I was going to make a last-minute decision, which of course meant I had not yet bought any of the ingredients. My late decision meant one thing: I was going to have to get out of my car. My dilemma was that I could make it easy on myself and drive to the local supermarket, where by parking as close as I could to the entrance the rain would hardly touch me, or I could drive to the local High Street. If I decided on the High Street I would have to keep my fingers crossed that I would find a parking space, then dash into the newsagent's to get some change for the parking meter and hope that I wouldn't end up in an argument with a traffic warden wanting to give me a ticket because I had been away from my car for two minutes.

Even if I managed to do all that, I would still have a long walk without an umbrella or raincoat. I may have found a hiding place from this awful weather but it had now put me in a position where my principles would be tested. Supermarket or local butcher? For most people given this dilemma there is only one choice – the supermarket. I too am happy to buy most of the ingredients I need from there, but the one vital ingredient for that evening's meal, the meat, I would only buy from my butcher.

# RICH BEEF HOT POT

This hearty and warming stew is perfect served with lots of creamy mashed potato to soak up the gravy. Serve with shredded cooked cabbage on the side and a large glass of red wine. This also freezes really well, so make a batch and freeze in individual portions. Then simply defrost and reheat in a pan on the hob until piping hot.

**serves 4**

1 tablespoon plain flour
650 g braising beef, cut into large cubes
3 tablespoons olive oil
1 onion, chopped
2 garlic cloves, crushed
2 large carrots, cut into thick batons
350 g celeriac, cut into thick batons
300 ml ginger wine
450 ml beef stock
2 tablespoons tomato purée
1 dried bouquet garni
salt and freshly ground black pepper

1. Preheat the oven to Gas Mark 4/180°C/fan oven 160°C. Put the flour on a plate and dust the beef in it, shaking off the excess. Heat half the oil in a flameproof casserole pan and cook the beef for 5 minutes, turning until brown all over. You will have to do this in batches. Remove and set aside.
2. Heat the remaining oil in the pan and add the onion, garlic, carrots and celeriac and cook gently for 5–8 minutes until starting to brown. Return the beef to the pan and add the ginger wine, beef stock, tomato purée and bouquet garni. Season generously. Bring to the boil, cover and cook in the oven for 2 hours until the meat is tender and the juices have reduced and thickened. Check the seasoning and serve.

# PAPRIKA AND GARLIC STEAKS

Once marinated, these steaks can be frozen in the freezer bags. Then when the sun shines and you fancy an impromptu alfresco dinner on the barbecue, simply defrost for a few hours and you're ready to go.

**serves 2**

2 rib eye steaks

**for the paprika and garlic paste**
½ onion, chopped
2 tablespoons paprika
1 tablespoon ground ginger
2 teaspoons turmeric
3 teaspoons garlic purée
1 fresh rosemary sprig, leaves only
4 tablespoons olive oil
1 tablespoon white wine vinegar

1. Put all the ingredients for the paprika and garlic paste into a small food processor and whizz until finely minced into a thick paste. Put the rib eye steaks into a freezer bag and add the paste. Seal and then massage the steaks from the outside until coated in the paste. Leave to marinate for at least 1 hour or in the fridge for up to 8 hours.
2. Bring the steaks back to room temperature. Remove the steaks from the marinade, discarding any excess paste with your hands. Heat a griddle pan until hot and cook the steaks for 3–4 minutes on each side, depending on the thickness of the steak, until medium. Transfer to a board and loosely cover with foil for 10 minutes before serving.

# BEEF
## with Cheat's Oyster Sauce

I've chosen to make my own oyster sauce using cooked mussels instead of oysters, which saves you the time it takes to shuck oysters. It produces a very similar but not as strong flavour, perfect for this dish. If you are short of time, you could use a bottle of good-quality oyster sauce instead and start from step 2, replacing the mussel sauce with oyster sauce. Add as much or as little as you like.

**serves 2**

40 g dried shiitake mushrooms

125 g cooked and shelled mussels

3 tablespoons light soy sauce

2 tablespoons dark soy sauce

1 teaspoon light muscovado sugar

2 tablespoons sake

300 g rump steak, thinly sliced

1 tablespoon cornflour

2 tablespoons groundnut oil

1 large carrot, thinly sliced

3 spring onions, cut into short lengths

1. Soak the dried mushrooms in boiling water for 20 minutes. Meanwhile, put the mussels, light and dark soy sauces, sugar, sake and 5 tablespoons cold water into a small lidded pan. Bring to the boil, cover and simmer for 10 minutes. Remove from the heat and whizz with a hand blender until smooth. Pass through a fine sieve into a jug and set aside. Discard the sediment.

2. Coat the steak in the cornflour and set aside. Drain the mushrooms, reserving 3 tablespoons of soaking liquid. Heat a large wok until hot and add the oil. Stir fry the beef for 2 minutes until browned, stirring continuously, then add the carrot, dried mushrooms and spring onions. Continue to stir fry for 2–3 minutes until the vegetables are softened but still retain some crunch.

3. Pour in the mussel sauce and reserved mushroom liquid and bubble for 1 minute till reduced and thickened. Serve immediately.

' I love the big bold flavour of oyster sauce, and the combination of this dark brown thick sauce with the beef is mouth-watering. '

In the last few years there has been much talk about the power of the supermarkets and how this power is killing off the small retail outlets on the High Street. Even though many people want to shop locally, the High Street experience is so stressful that they give up – regardless of good or bad weather. Consumers have been deserting the High Street for the supermarket because they provide stress-free parking, everything under one roof and, with the aid of modern psychological techniques, stores laid out to our convenience.

For small local High Street retailers, everything is stacked against them. As well as parking issues, they can't compete with the buying power of the supermarkets. It is clear for everyone to see when they walk along their High Streets that most of the small independent retailers have disappeared. Many bakeries and greengrocers have closed as supermarkets bring those services in-house.

I don't want to slag off supermarkets because they are a huge part of our culture and I have a number of my products listed in their stores, but I do see that they have an overwhelming advantage over small suppliers and that they also now determine what most people eat in the home. Supermarkets undoubtedly give you convenience, but the price we pay for that convenience is, oddly enough, lack of choice.

Supermarkets are a volume-based business. It is better to sell more of the same rather than offer too much selection. For example, we have 100 different varieties of apple that could be grown in this country but you would be lucky if you can five different varieties in the supermarket. With the supermarkets dominating the food chain they are deciding what most of us put on our table to eat. Nearly every product that was once sold in the High Street can now be found in the supermarket, but they are not getting it all their own way. An area of the supermarket that they can't get right and where they can't steal customers is the butchery. Consumers still feel that they will get a much better product and service from an independent butcher.

A good butcher is as important as your doctor, teacher or policeman. Because I often find myself between London, Chippenham and Devon I am lucky to have more than one. Going to see my London butcher is like watching an artist at work. There is often a long queue at his shop because the meat is cut, boned, trimmed and tied there in front of you. My London butcher is always very pleased to offer up recipe suggestions, some of which inspired me to write the following recipes using different cuts of steak.

# TANGY BEEF KEBABS

Tamarind is also known as the Indian date and is in fact the secret ingredient in Worcestershire sauce. A tangy tart fruit, you can find it as a paste in the herbs and spices section of the supermarket.

**serves 2**

3 tablespoons agave nectar (see tip)
2 tablespoons chilli garlic sauce or peri peri sauce
2 tablespoons tamarind paste
¼ teaspoon ground cumin
zest and juice of ½ orange
1 tablespoon finely chopped fresh coriander
2 tablespoons olive oil
350 g sirloin steaks, cut into even cubes

1. Put the agave nectar, chilli garlic sauce, tamarind paste, cumin, orange zest and juice, coriander and olive oil into a large freezer bag. Add the sirloin steak cubes and seal the bag tightly. Massage the steak through the bag to coat in the marinade. Leave to marinate for up to 8 hours.
2. Preheat the grill or barbecue to hot. Thread the steak on to four metal or soaked wooden skewers, discarding the marinade. Cook the kebabs for 5–6 minutes, turning until the steak is starting to char and is cooked – they will still be a bit pink in the middle. Cook for a few minutes longer if you want them well done. Serve immediately.

**tip** Agave nectar is a natural fructose sweetener extracted from the agave plant. You can find it with the sugar alternatives in the supermarket, but you could use runny honey if you wish.

# STEAK IN SHERRY SAUCE

If you have the time, leave the strips of steak to marinate in the paprika and allspice for at least an hour for a more intense flavour.

**serves 4**

600 g sirloin steak, cut into thin strips
2 teaspoons paprika
1 teaspoon ground allspice
2 tablespoons olive oil
25 g butter
3 banana shallots, finely sliced
1 garlic clove, crushed
125 ml dry sherry
300 ml single cream
2 tablespoons mushroom ketchup
salt and freshly ground black pepper

1. Put the steak strips into a non-metallic bowl and add the paprika, allspice and lots of black pepper. Toss to coat thoroughly and set aside.
2. Heat half the oil in a large heavy-based frying pan and cook half the steak strips for 2–3 minutes, turning until browned. Remove and set aside. Repeat with the remaining oil and steak. Remove and set aside. Drain any oil from the pan.
3. Melt the butter in the same pan and gently cook the shallots and garlic for 5 minutes until softened. Add the sherry and bubble rapidly for 5 minutes, until reduced. Pour in the single cream and mushroom ketchup and bring to a simmer, stirring. Bubble for a few minutes until reduced and slightly thickened. Check the seasoning and return the browned steak and juices to the pan. Bubble for 1–2 minutes to heat through, then serve immediately.

If I bought my meat from a supermarket instead of my butcher it would feel as if I were abandoning an old friend: someone who is always there to offer advice on what to cook for dinner when I need inspiration, who is always ready to prepare the meat to my special specification and always able to give me some bones – an essential for a good stock. All my friend expects in return is that I resist the temptation of going to the supermarket to buy meat. The long-term survival of my butcher and others like him is going to depend on the consumer resisting the supermarket butcher's counter, even if it occasionally means getting a drenching in the process. So, like my old friend the butcher, here is another close friend, Roast Beef and Yorkshire Puddings. Without which, the dark winter months wouldn't have flown by so quickly.

# ROAST BEEF

## and Yorkshire Puddings

This recipe is very simple due to the fact that all the flavours come from the joint of beef. Cooking a roast on the bone, such as the rib, gives the meat the most wonderful flavour and juices. If you wanted to jazz it up, then brush the top of the beef with whole grain mustard for the last 30 minutes, but for me the integrity of the beef shouldn't be messed with.

**serves 6, with leftovers**

3.25 kg prime rib of beef on the bone
2 tablespoons olive oil
salt and freshly ground black pepper

**for the Yorkshire puddings**
125 g plain flour
3 eggs, beaten
200 ml full fat milk
75 g beef dripping

**for the gravy**
100 ml red wine
1 tablespoon plain flour
300 ml beef stock

1. Preheat the oven to Gas Mark 6/200°C/fan oven 180°C. Put the rib of beef into a large roasting tin and rub over the oil. Season generously and roast in the oven for 20 minutes.

2. Meanwhile, make the Yorkshire pudding batter. Put the flour into a bowl and make a well in the centre. Season and then pour the eggs into the well. Whisk the mixture from the centre, slowly incorporating the eggs, and then gradually pour in the milk while whisking, until a smooth batter is formed. Set aside.

3. Reduce the oven temperature to Gas Mark 4/180°C/fan oven 160°C and baste the beef with the pan juices. Continue to roast in the oven for 1¾ hours for medium-done beef. If you like it a little rarer cook for 15 minutes less, and for well done cook for 15 minutes more.

4. Transfer to a board, loosely cover with foil and set aside to rest. Increase the oven temperature to Gas Mark 7/220°C/ fan oven 200°C and divide the beef dripping between the sections of a 12-hole bun tin. Put into the oven for 5 minutes. Whisk the batter one last time and then transfer to a jug. Remove the bun tin from the oven and carefully pour the batter into each hole. Bake in the oven for 15 minutes until golden and risen.

5. Meanwhile, drain any excess fat from the roasting tin and return to the hob. Add half the red wine and bubble rapidly until well reduced while scraping the residue from the bottom of the pan with a wooden spoon. Sprinkle with the flour and cook for 1 minute, continuously stirring. Add the remaining red wine and the stock and bring to a simmer. Gently cook for 2–3 minutes until thickened and reduced. Check seasoning and keep warm.

6. Carve the beef and serve with the Yorkshire puddings, gravy and all the trimmings.

# SPICED POT ROAST

Although classed as old-fashioned, I love this method of cooking. Slowly roasting and braising at the same time means the end result is incredibly juicy and tender. Serve with creamy mashed or puréed cannellini beans and cooked baby carrots.

**serves 6**

2.25 kg brisket or silverside beef
300 ml red wine
50 g beef dripping
2 onions, roughly chopped
2 tablespoons tomato purée
a small handful of fresh thyme
2 bay leaves
150 ml beef stock
1 tablespoon plain flour
1 tablespoon butter

**for the spice mix**
2 tablespoons curry powder
1 teaspoon celery salt
1 teaspoon paprika
1 teaspoon ground mixed spice
2 tablespoons soy sauce
2 garlic cloves, crushed
freshly ground black pepper

1. In a small bowl mix together the ingredients for the spice mix to make a paste, seasoning generously with black pepper. Put the beef on a board and unroll. Cut the joint down the centre, leaving it still attached, and open out like a book.

2. Spread the spice mix over the meat, then roll back up and tie securely in about five places. Put the beef in a large bowl and cover with the red wine. Leave to marinate for at least 4 hours, turning halfway through.

3. Preheat the oven to Gas Mark 3/160°C/fan oven 140°C. Remove the beef from the red wine and dry with kitchen paper. Reserve the red wine. Melt the dripping in a large flameproof lidded casserole pan and heat until hot. Add the beef and cook for 5 minutes, turning until brown all over. Remove and set aside.

4. Add the onions to the pan and continue to cook for 10 minutes, until softened and starting to brown. Stir in the tomato purée and cook for 1 minute. Then stir in the reserved red wine, the thyme, bay leaves and beef stock. Return the beef to the pan and bring to the boil.

5. Cover tightly and cook in the oven for 2 hours. Remove the meat and set aside for 15 minutes, loosely covered in foil. Meanwhile, strain the cooking liquor and return to the pan. Mix together the flour and butter. Bring the cooking liquor to the boil and then whisk in the butter paste. Cook for 1 minute, stirring until thickened. Carve the beef and serve with the gravy.

' I am especially keen for you to try the cuts that take a bit longer to cook as you will not only be giving yourself a real treat but you will be helping the likes of Phillip Warren to make their business work. For he and butchers like him need to be able to sell the whole carcass to make butchering viable. '

There are people that we meet on life's journey who can play a pivotal role in helping us become who we want to be, without necessarily realizing the impact they have on our lives. It is as if these people have been sent by the gods to clear a path through life's ups and downs and to point us in the right direction. I have been lucky enough in my life to have met several of these people. One such person to whom I would like to pay tribute comes in the guise of a rotund, rosy-cheeked, weather-beaten West Countryman.

Although he probably isn't aware of it, Phillip Warren of Warren's butchers in Launceston, Cornwall, had a big impact on my deciding to produce beef cattle. What this man doesn't know about beef isn't worth knowing. It was some ten years ago that I met Phillip, when I first bought my farm. In those days I was very wet behind the ears when it came to information about beef. I didn't know or care about how beef was reared, selected or matured. To my amazement, Phillip's passion for good-quality meat in general and beef in particular was on a par with a Master of Wine. He treats every cut of beef as if it were a fine bottle of claret.

The first thing that amazed me when I went to his shop was that he made a big deal of highlighting the different breeds of animal that the cuts come from. The farmer who had reared the animal was named for all the customers to see as though in honour of all his hard work. Customers had the names and addresses of all the farmers who were producing their food – real direct access. I wasn't surprised to see that some years later the supermarkets cottoned on to that idea and started to put pictures of farmers on their own-label products. Somehow the supermarkets' attempts at doing this don't work so well, as it feels like a badge job, with farmers doing this as part of their contract with the supermarket rather than in genuine partnership. For with a genuine partnership comes an equal voice. In Warren's shop carcasses hang like prized trophies. It feels like a place of reverence rather than one of trade, like going into one of those haute couture shops in Knightsbridge in London. If you are accustomed to the sterile supermarket environment, where the meat is neatly packaged, seeing this amazing display is a delight to the senses.

Modern-day methods of selling meat go to great lengths to 'protect' the consumer from the whole process of rearing meat. The result being that many people have little understanding of the hard work that goes into producing a great-tasting cut of meat and lack knowledge of what to look for when buying meat. The good people of Launceston, however, know that preparing a great meal starts at Warren's and not on the kitchen table. Fair weather or foul, there's no dilemma here between the supermarket or the butcher.

If the front of Phillip Warren's shop tantalized, then the back gave my senses an experience that has forever been imprinted on my mind – so much so, it became the trigger for me to keep beef cattle. At the back of Warren's shop is an army of butchers dedicated to preparing different cuts of meat. As I toured this wonderland I was in awe of the skill that these butchers possess. Like my London butcher, this brigade have such artistry about them I would have been happy to pay money to watch them perform.

When the doors of the massive fridges were opened, I was blasted with cold air, which ensured that I was fully alert to what I was about to see next – full-sized Ruby Red beef carcasses. This was the first time that I had ever seen a whole carcass, and I was struck by the size of them. Majestically these carcasses stood out, gleaming with pride at the pleasure they were about to give the eater. It needed two people to take a carcass off its hook and lay it on the table for the master to begin his work dissecting. As Phillip went about his craft he gave me a master class on how the animal needed to be reared and finished to get it to this end stage.

For Phillip, the farmer who keeps the animal, and how it has been fed, is so important that he will go and see every beast before it ends up in his shop. He discusses with the farmer the precise day the animal should be sent off to slaughter and then determines the right amount of time that each carcass should be hung before it is ready for his knife. Cutting away at the carcass I was taught the names of all the cuts of meat, which I have listed here, together with a diagram that you may find helpful the next time you visit your butcher.

**BRISKET OR THICK FLANK** Both these cuts are perfect for pot roasting, stewing or braising. Try Spiced Pot Roast (page 104).

**SHIN** This tough cut is best slowly casseroled or braised.

**TOPSIDE/TOP RUMP** These are two overlapping muscles and the top rump is slightly more tender. They both should be slow roasted – ideal for pot roasting, stewing or braising.

**SILVERSIDE** This joint is a large lean muscle as it mainly does all the work. It may be slow roasted with added fat for an economical roast, but braising or pot roasting give a far better end result.

**RUMP** Must be well matured for a flavoursome steak. Can be grilled, pan fried or barbecued, and makes a quick supper when cut into strips and stir fried. Try Beef with Cheat's Oyster Sauce (page 96).

**SIRLOIN** Perfect for grilling or frying as a tender succulent steak, such as in Tangy Beef Kebabs (page 99) and Steak in Sherry Sauce (page 99), but don't get confused as this is also a whole joint, ideal for roasting.

**FILLET** This is one of the most expensive cuts of beef because it is so tender. When cut into steaks it is great for pan frying, or fast roast it whole. Try to keep the fillet medium-rare as it loses all its flavour if overcooked. Why not try Oriental Beef Wellington (page 115)?

**FORE RIB** This, in my mind, is the ideal roasting joint, as the fat and bones help to flavour and keep the joint juicy during cooking, a bit like self-basting, see Roast Beef and Yorkshire Puddings (page 101). Often this joint is cut to make rib eye steaks, perfect for grilling or frying. See Paprika and Garlic Steaks (page 93) or Jamaican Patties (page 116).

**CHUCK** Often sold as braising, stewing or feather steak. This meat needs long slow cooking. Very economical, and when cooked right it simply melts in the mouth. Check out Slow-Cooked Rendang Curry (page 108), Rich Beef Hot Pot (page 93) and Trieste-Style Beef Goulash (page 113).

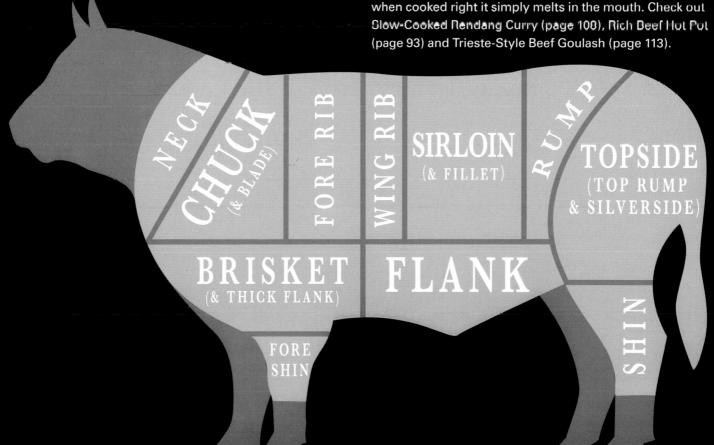

## SLOW-COOKED RENDANG CURRY

Feather steak is so called because of the feather-like blade of fat that runs along the meat. You could use any other cut that is suitable for braising.

**serves 4**

2 tablespoons sunflower oil
750 g feather steak, cut into small chunks
400 ml coconut milk
2 star anise
toasted coconut flakes and a small handful of
    coriander leaves to serve

**for the Rendang paste**
1 onion, chopped
4 garlic cloves, chopped
1 tablespoon ground ginger
1 tablespoon tamarind paste
4 tablespoons guava jam
2 tablespoons Thai fish sauce
1 teaspoon turmeric
1 tablespoon jerk seasoning paste
1½ tablespoons garam masala

1. Put all the ingredients for the Rendang paste into a small food processor and whizz to form a paste. Set aside.

2. Heat the oil in a large saucepan and cook the feather steak for 5 minutes, turning until brown all over. You will have to do this in batches.

3. Return all the steak to the pan and stir in the Rendang paste. Cook for 1 minute, stirring. Pour in the coconut milk and add the star anise. Bring to the boil, then lower the heat and simmer gently for 1–1½ hours, until the meat is tender and the sauce is really thick and coating the meat. Serve immediately topped with coconut flakes and coriander.

## OXTAIL STEW

The meat from oxtail is lean but surrounded by a layer of fat, which should be trimmed before cooking. Ask your butcher to cut the tail into short lengths for you.

**serves 4**

3 tablespoons olive oil
1 oxtail (approx 1 kg), cut into short lengths
2 onions, finely sliced
3 carrots, chopped
2 garlic cloves, finely chopped
450 ml dry cider
1 tablespoon plain flour
1 tablespoon sun-dried tomato purée
600 ml beef stock
2 tablespoons grated horseradish
1 dudhi, peeled and chopped (see tip)
salt and freshly ground black pepper

1. Heat half the oil in a flameproof casserole pan and cook the oxtail for 5 minutes, turning until brown all over. You will have to do this in batches. Remove and set aside. Add the remaining oil and cook the onions, carrots and garlic for 5–8 minutes until starting to soften and brown.

2. Add the cider and allow to bubble for a few minutes. Stir in the flour and tomato purée and cook for 1 minute, stirring. Gradually pour in the beef stock until smooth and combined. Return the oxtail pieces, season and bring to the boil. Cover and simmer on a low heat for 3 hours.

3. Stir in the grated horseradish and dudhi. Cover again and simmer for a further 30 minutes, until the sauce has thickened and the oxtail falls off the bone. Check the seasoning and serve immediately.

**tip** Dudhi is a marrow-like vegetable from India. It can be found in ethnic stores or some large supermarkets.

I left Phillip Warren's butcher's shop sure that I wanted to keep beef cattle on my farm and that I wanted something special. I wished to produce a breed that is indigenous to the region rather than go for cattle that were not part of Devon's heritage. I decided on the North Devon breed, also known as Ruby Reds. It is a breed of cattle from the south-west of England. In recent years it has fallen out of favour, as more rapidly growing Continental breeds are in demand because of their speed of maturity. In my view, the meat from these Continental breeds is of lower quality and inferior to the slower-maturing grass-fed North Devon traditional breeds.

The gentle-natured North Devons with their warm coats are extremely hardy, which means you can keep them outside pretty much all winter. Low maintenance, easy handling and the ability to fatten almost wholly on grass give them an advantage over the larger breeds.

Beef from Ruby Red Devon cattle is very tender, well marbled and full flavoured. The meat should be hung for a minimum of three weeks, which reduces the water content and produces the darker colour meat. This, along with the marbling, produces the full flavour and tenderness that make Red Ruby Devon beef very tasty. I am pleased to say that the Ruby Red is regaining popularity and more and more farmers are

returning to rearing this breed. With places like Warren's that celebrate the farmer and good-quality meats, I live in hope that the Ruby Red breed will one day challenge the Aberdeen Angus as the best-quality beef.

When I go into Warren's now I always feel a great sense of satisfaction and pride that my name is also on his board, for customers to see. For me it says I have made the grade and my beef has met with his approval to adorn this temple of great-quality produce. Since those early days ten years ago, things on the High Street have got tougher and I have watched Launceston town centre go gradually downhill as other small retailers have left. Warren's sticks out as a ray of hope against this decline, offering fine traditional local produce, great service and a passion for the butcher's craft.

As the days get shorter before the winter sets in, we get a lot of rain in my part of Devon. From where my farm is, you get plenty of warning that the storm clouds are mustering. Rain symbolizes change, new beginnings and hope. My hope is that Phillip Warren and his like don't get washed away by the ever-more-powerful supermarkets and that somehow we find a way for them to co-exist. So I can't really finish this chapter without offering up some recipes that were inspired by my love of the West Country, all that is traditional, and flavours from around the globe.

We are local farmers & Butchers carrying on
probably the oldest farm shop in Cornwall. We
work with about 130 like-minded small farmers
producing natural meat from pasture on the
margins of Dartmoor & Bodmin Moors, reared
naturally in the traditional way.

THE LOCAL FARMERS SUPPLYING US THIS WEEK

WERRINGTON PARK ~ RED DEVON

DAVID THOMAS ~ KENNARDS HOUSE ~ SOUTH DEVON x RED ANGUS

ANDREW GOOD ~ BADHARLICK RED HEREFORD

These two recipes have a distinct Italian influence thanks to my brother-in-law, Michael Scott, who has generously shared them with me.

## TRIESTE-STYLE BEEF GOULASH

Diced shin also works really well in this dish, but you may need to cook it a little longer until the meat is tender. If the sauce starts to reduce too much, just add a splash of stock.

serves 4–6

2 tablespoons olive oil
800 g braising or stewing steak, cut into large pieces
2 onions, finely chopped
2 tablespoons tomato purée
1 tablespoon smoked paprika
1 fresh rosemary sprig, leaves finely chopped
a small handful of fresh oregano leaves
1 bay leaf
150 ml dry white wine
400 g can plum tomatoes
2 tablespoons kalamata olive tapenade
salt and freshly ground black pepper

1. Heat the oil in a large flameproof casserole pan and cook the beef for 5 minutes, turning until brown. Remove and set aside. You will need to do this in batches. Add the onions and cook for 5–8 minutes until softened and just starting to brown.
2. Return the beef and stir in the tomato purée and paprika. Cook for 1 minute, stirring, then stir in the rosemary, nearly all the oregano leaves, the bay leaf, white wine and tomatoes. Bring to the boil, then cover and simmer for 1½ hours, or until the beef is tender and the sauce has thickened.
3. Check the seasoning and serve immediately in shallow bowls, topped with a spoonful of tapenade and a few oregano leaves.

## GRANDMA'S ITALIAN MEATBALLS

These meatballs are delicious served in a tomato sauce such as Sweet and Spicy Tomato Sauce (page 177) or tossed with pasta, such as linguine, with lemon juice and finely chopped herbs.

serves 4

500 g lean steak mince
1 egg, beaten
50 g Parmesan cheese, finely grated
60 g fresh breadcrumbs
2 tablespoons finely chopped fresh flat-leaf parsley
2 garlic cloves, crushed
zest and juice of ½ lemon
½ teaspoon freshly grated nutmeg
2 teaspoons dried Italian mixed herbs
2 tablespoons olive oil
salt and freshly ground black pepper

1. Put the mince into a large bowl and add the egg, Parmesan, breadcrumbs, parsley, garlic, lemon zest and juice, nutmeg and dried herbs. Season generously and then mix well with your hands, kneading until combined.
2. With wet hands roll the mixture into 24 small balls, slightly flattening them so they are not perfectly round.
3. Heat the oil in a frying pan and cook the meatballs for 15 minutes until cooked through and golden brown all over. Serve immediately.

# ORIENTAL BEEF WELLINGTON

Suitably named after the first Duke of Wellington, according to some sources, this version has a fusion of Eastern and Western flavours, which complement the rich fillet of beef remarkably well.

**serves 4–6**

3 tablespoons olive oil

800 g piece of beef fillet

120 g shiitake mushrooms, trimmed and really finely chopped

140 g exotic mushroom selection, trimmed and really finely chopped

2 tablespoons sweet white miso paste

10 Parma ham slices

100 g mushroom pâté

2–3 tablespoons plain flour

500 g pack puff pastry

1 egg, beaten

Sichuan pepper to season

1. Season the beef all over with the pepper. Heat half the oil in a frying pan and sear the beef on all sides for 5 minutes until brown all over. Remove and set aside. Heat the remaining oil in the pan and gently fry the shiitake and exotic mushrooms for 5 minutes until the mushrooms are starting to lightly brown and the liquid has evaporated. Stir in the miso paste, season with more pepper if needed and take off the heat. The mixture should come together. Leave to cool.

2. Lay a large sheet of clingfilm on a clean surface. Arrange the slices of Parma ham in a rectangle on the clingfilm, each one slightly overlapping the last. Using a palette knife, spread the mushroom pâté over the Parma ham in a thin layer. Then spread the cooled mushroom mixture on top.

3. Place the beef fillet along one long edge of the Parma ham. Using the clingfilm to help, carefully roll the beef fillet up in the Parma ham and mushrooms. Twist the clingfilm at the ends and chill the beef for 15 minutes.

4. Dust a clean surface with flour and roll the pastry into a large rectangle and until it is 5 mm thick. Carefully unwrap the beef fillet and discard the clingfilm. Put the beef in the centre of the pastry. Brush any exposed pastry with the beaten egg and then wrap the pastry around the beef, trimming the ends and sealing tightly. Place on a baking tray, seam side down, and chill for 30 minutes.

5. Preheat the oven to Gas Mark 6/200°C/fan oven 180°C. Brush the pastry all over with the remaining beaten egg. Bake in the oven for 35–40 minutes. Leave to rest for 10 minutes before carving into thick slices and serving.

# JAMAICAN PATTIES

These are inspired by the Cornish pasty, but with a huge Jamaican twist.

**makes 8**

**for the pastry**

500 g plain flour
150 g chilled butter, cut into cubes
80 g chilled lard, cut into cubes
2 teaspoons turmeric
a generous pinch of salt

**for the filling**

300 g rib eye steak, excess fat removed and cut into
   small chunks
½ onion, finely chopped
2 tablespoons dried breadcrumbs
1 tomato, deseeded and finely diced
1 heaped tablespoon jerk seasoning paste
150 g sweet potato, peeled and cut into 5 mm thick
   slices
2 tablespoons full fat milk

1. To make the pastry, put the flour, butter, lard, turmeric and salt into a food processor and whizz until it resembles fine breadcrumbs. Gradually add 4–5 tablespoons cold water, pulsing between each addition until it forms a soft but not sticky dough. Empty out on to a surface lightly dusted with flour and gently knead to bring together. Wrap in clingfilm and chill in the fridge for 30 minutes.

2. Meanwhile, to make the filling mix together the steak, onion, breadcrumbs, tomato and jerk seasoning in a bowl until combined. Set aside.

3. Unwrap the pastry. Dust the surface with a little more flour and roll out the pastry until it is about 5 mm thick. Using a saucer as a guide, cut out eight circles. You will have to re-roll the pastry.

4. Preheat the oven to Gas Mark 4/180°C/fan oven 160°C. Put two slices of sweet potato on one half of a pastry circle, leaving a 1 cm border. Top with a spoonful of the meat filling and then brush the pastry edges with water. Fold over the other half of the pastry to make a pasty, half moon in shape. Using a fork, press the edges to seal, making a pattern. Repeat, to make eight pasties in total.

5. Transfer the pasties to a non-stick baking tray and arrange spaced apart. Brush all over with milk then, using a skewer, make two steam holes in the top of each pasty. Bake in the oven for 1 hour or until lightly golden and cooked. Leave to cool for 10 minutes before eating.

' These are also great cold and are the perfect portable food. If you like it hot then add a touch more jerk seasoning for a real kick. '

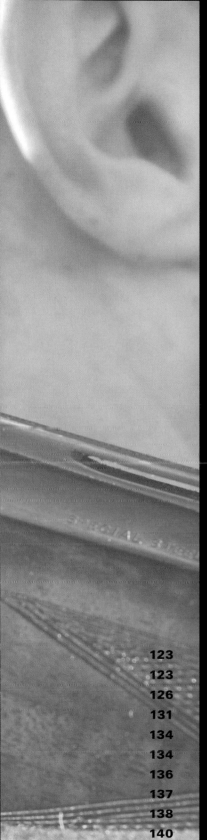

# GAME,
## OFFAL AND VEAL

'**P**ull,' I shouted. 'Now control your breathing. Hold her firmly. When you have it in your sights, squeeeeze. She's unforgiving. If you're not gentle with her she'll give you such a kick you won't forget it in a hurry.' My words are uttered in a calm, slow manner, deliberately done so as to counter my excitement. After many failed attempts I know that I have to get myself under control. This is easier said than done because everything around is conspiring against me.

I have got nine youngsters staying with me on my farm – all from inner cities around the country (page 128–129). These are the youngsters that I have selected to take part in The Black Farmer Rural Scholarship scheme. The idea is for them to experience working and living in rural Britain – none has ever been in the countryside before. For four weeks these youngsters – ranging in age from seventeen to twenty-five – will live and breathe the rural life. Most importantly they will get away from the white noise of city living, where they are constantly bombarded with stimuli – a constant barrage against the senses. I want them to experience the slower pace of country living, a pace that may help them connect with who they are rather than who they think they should be and so, perhaps, make better choices in life.

Many of these youngsters had been dealt some pretty poor cards in life and were heading for a future on society's discard pile. As a great believer that environment can be a cause of many of the ills in society, I felt that a change of environment was maybe what these young people needed.

My approach with these young people was tough love, to somehow try and get through to them that they could turn their lives around if they really wanted to. Rather than blame society for their lot in life I wanted the time they spent on the farm to be an opportunity to look at how they could change their lives. I felt that they would be able to see that with determination and focus they too could achieve their dreams.

As a young boy growing up in inner-city Birmingham I had the same start as many of these youngsters. I knew that if they had the courage to hope and dream it was possible to change their future. Although I dreamt of owning a farm when I was a kid I daren't put up my hand in the classroom to share my ambition for fear of being laughed at. Even if I'd had the courage to describe my dream, the teachers at an inner-city school like mine would have been at a loss to know what they could do to help me gain experience.

So, when I bought my farm, one thing I was immediately keen to do was offer inner-city youngsters the opportunity to experience farming. And here I was with my first year's intake and for the first time in my life handling a shotgun. Tonight, pheasant and venison were on the menu. It was outside the season but I still wanted them to experience shooting. As I desperately tried to control my breathing they did everything they could possibly think of to put me off. The previous three weeks had been very hard on the youngsters; for the first time in their lives they had to adhere to some strict discipline, hard work and a change of environment. Today they could relax and let their hair down a little and they were going to make good use of the opportunity.

Just as I had managed to get my excitement and breathing under control, they lined up the clays into my sight. Following my tutor's instructions I squeezed the trigger gently. Just at that moment the comedian of the group came up with a wisecrack, well timed to synchronize with the squeezing of the trigger. I unloaded my barrel at the clays and the accompanying roar of laughter signalled that I had missed my target yet again. I decided I was no marksman and extricated myself from the relentless ribbing by returning to my cooking.

I have been asked on a couple of occasions to go on a shoot, but I have always declined. **I think the knowledge of my hopeless shooting ability is best kept between my Black Farmer Scholarship students and me.** Pheasant has the image of being a posh person's dish and many people feel that it isn't the meat for them. This image derives from the elitism of pheasant shooting as a sport. During the season very wealthy urbanites regularly try to impress their clients by taking them on very expensive shoots. The more expensive the shoot the more prestige it seems to hold. I have heard that a top-end shoot can cost around £5000 per gun or more.

But with all this talk about pheasant we mustn't forget guinea fowl. This small gamey bird is neither totally wild nor domesticated but has been reared since Elizabethan times. Its flavour is a cross between pheasant and chicken and is also finger-licking good. Both pheasant and guinea fowl are versatile birds and can be roasted whole, pan fried as portions or diced in casseroles. The following recipes are great ways of cooking these little birds and are so simple that they are no way scary if this is your first experience with either bird.

# PHEASANT
## cooked in Madeira

Serve this creamy dish with cooked tenderstem broccoli and peas. If you don't fancy using pheasant then this also works really well with chicken or guinea fowl.

serves 4

12 shallots
2 tablespoons olive oil
2 pheasants, cut into portions
1 teaspoon caraway seeds, lightly crushed
½ teaspoon ground mace
1 tablespoon plain flour
300 ml chicken stock
150 ml dry white wine
75 ml Madeira
150 ml double cream
2 tablespoons chopped fresh tarragon
salt and freshly ground black pepper

1. Preheat the oven to Gas Mark 3/160°C/fan oven 140°C. Put the shallots in a bowl and cover with boiling water. Set aside. Heat the oil in a large lidded flameproof casserole pan and cook the pheasant pieces for 5 minutes until browned all over. You will need to do this in batches. Remove and set aside. Take the pan off the heat.
2. Drain the shallots then peel and cut in half. Return the pan to the heat and cook the shallots for 5–8 minutes until starting to soften and brown. Stir in the caraway seeds and mace and cook for 1 minute. Then add the flour and cook for 1 minute, stirring constantly. Gradually pour in the stock, wine and Madeira and stir until smooth and combined.
3. Return the pheasant to the pan, season generously and bring to a simmer. Cover and cook in the oven for 1 hour or until the pheasant is tender. Remove the casserole from the oven and take off the lid. Place the pan back on the hob and stir in the cream and tarragon. Bring to a simmer and bubble gently for 10–15 minutes until thickened. Check the seasoning and serve immediately.

# LIMONCELLO AND CHILLI ROASTED GUINEA FOWL

Originally from the west African coast these scrawny-looking birds can dry out quickly. Make sure you baste during cooking.

serves 2

150 ml limoncello
1 scotch bonnet chilli, finely chopped
zest and juice of 1 lime
1 tablespoon coriander seeds, crushed
2 tablespoons olive oil
1 kg guinea fowl
1 onion, halved
200 ml crème fraîche
salt and freshly ground black pepper

1. In a jug mix together the limoncello, chilli, lime zest and juice, coriander seeds and olive oil. Season generously. Put the guinea fowl into a large freezer bag and pour over the limoncello mixture. Seal the bag tightly and turn the bag upside down to coat the guinea fowl in the mixture. Leave to marinate for at least an hour or up to 8 hours in the fridge, turning regularly.
2. Preheat the oven to Gas Mark 5/190°C/fan oven 170°C. Remove the guinea fowl from the freezer bag and put into a roasting tin breast side down. Put the halved onion into the cavity of the bird and pour over the leftover marinade from the bag. Cover with foil and roast in the oven for 1 hour, basting a couple of times during cooking until the guinea fowl is cooked and the juices run clear.
3. Transfer the guinea fowl to a board, cover with foil and leave to rest for 10 minutes. Pour the roasting tin juices into a jug, leave to settle for a few minutes then discard the fat. Return the tin to the hob and pour in the tin juices. Bring to the boil, scraping any sediment from the bottom of the tin with a wooden spoon. Stir in the crème fraîche and bring to a simmer. Check the seasoning and keep warm. Carve the guinea fowl and serve with the creamy gravy.

The final two feathered game are pigeon and quail, the smallest of the game birds. Don't be afraid, the dark purple meat of pigeon is delicious served slightly pink, while the slightly gamey quail is similar to chicken. The following recipes are a great introduction to both these birds.

## PAN-FRIED PIGEON BREASTS
### with Wild Mushrooms and Truffle

The secret to cooking pigeon is to cook it quickly and then leave it to rest. This is a simple supper made in minutes and goes really well with creamy parsnip mash.

**serves 4**

8 pigeon breasts
2 tablespoons olive oil
2 fresh rosemary sprigs, leaves only
1 red onion, cut into thin wedges
25 g butter
200 g mixed wild mushrooms
1 whole black summer truffle, thinly sliced
75 ml dry white wine
4 teaspoons truffle oil
salt and freshly ground black pepper

1. Season the pigeon breasts and set aside. Heat the olive oil and rosemary leaves in a heavy-based frying pan until the rosemary starts to sizzle. Add the pigeon breasts and cook for 2–3 minutes on each side until just cooked. Remove to a board and loosely cover with foil. You will need to do this in batches.

2. Add the red onion to the rosemary oil and gently cook for 3–4 minutes until starting to soften. Then add the butter and gently heat until melted. Stir in the mushrooms and truffle slices and cook gently for a further 2–3 minutes until cooked and starting to brown.

3. Pour in the wine and let it bubble for a minute or so until reduced. Season generously and divide between warmed plates. Top each serving with two pigeon breasts, drizzle with the truffle oil and serve immediately.

# LIME AND POMEGRANATE QUAIL

These are one of the smallest breeds of poultry.

**serves 2**

4 quails
1 teaspoon rock salt
1 teaspoon dried pomegranate seeds
2 tablespoons pomegranate molasses
2 limes
1 onion, chopped
4 tablespoons olive oil
freshly ground black pepper

1. Take one quail and place on a board breast side down. With a pair of sharp scissors and starting at the cavity end, carefully snip each side of the backbone towards the neck. Remove the backbone and innards and rinse under a running tap. Dry with kitchen paper and then place on the board breast side up. With the palm of your hand press down on the breastbone until it cracks and the quail is flattened. Repeat with the remaining quails.

2. Put the salt and pomegranate seeds into a mortar and pestle and crush. Transfer to a large freezer bag and add the molasses, the zest of one of the limes and the juice of both, the onion and olive oil. Season with black pepper and add the birds. Seal the bag and massage to ensure the quails are coated in the marinade. Set aside for at least 4 hours.

3. When ready to cook remove the quails from the bag and discard the marinade. Place a quail on a board breast side up and thread a metal or soaked wooden skewer through the neck end, passing through the wings. Thread another skewer below the breast, passing through the legs. Repeat with the remaining quails.

4. Preheat the grill or barbecue until hot. Cook the quails for 12–15 minutes, turning until cooked and the juices run clear. Serve immediately.

' These succulent little birds are ideal for barbecuing. '

Having tried and failed in my army career, I spent several years working as a chef. In my spare time I would watch films or television, but the voice within me convinced me that I didn't have to be an observer and gave me the confidence to become part of the world of television. I wanted to make programmes that would inspire people. I wanted to make programmes that would make a difference to people's lives. This was all well and good, but my ambition had a number of major drawbacks. Most programme-makers then came from the top universities in the country and with my dyslexia I had the disadvantage of hardly being able to read and write. I had set myself a tall ask.

The gods may not have furnished me with a brain that allowed me to pass exams, but they compensated with gifts that far outweigh that: determination and focus. Armed with these I spent eighteen months badgering anyone who would listen for a job in television. Although on paper it looked as if I was not the right person to work in television, I managed to find someone who was prepared to take a chance with me.

I started off as a researcher and eventually became a director. I worked on a variety of programmes but eventually found my natural home, working on food programmes. The gods rewarded me for all my hard work and I got to travel the world making programmes on the subject of food and drink.

I first got my taste for venison on a trip to South Africa over twenty years ago. While I was working at the BBC I was fortunate enough to be sent to Cape Town to make a film about the burgeoning South African wine industry. It was just after Nelson Mandela's release from prison and the country had a real air of optimism and pride. It is a beautiful country with some great wines and great food. The South Africans are big meat-eaters and they especially like game – often cooked on a barbecue.

Venison is well known for being low in fat. That is all well and good for the health-conscious, but fat in all meats is a very important component to the meat being tasty. When preparing venison, more often than not it will require additional fat. This could be anything from bacon to olive oil or other meats. For those of you who have never tried venison before, the best introduction is to try either a venison sausage or burger. The following recipe for Venison and Caramelized Onion Burgers is quick and easy. Once you have mastered this, move on to the Venison Fillet with Pine Nut Stuffing and Cassis Sauce for a show-off dinner menu.

## VENISON AND CARAMELIZED ONION BURGERS

These burgers freeze really well – simply layer between squares of parchment paper and then wrap in foil before freezing. Defrost thoroughly before cooking.

**serves 6**

3 Black Farmer Premium pork sausages
500 g venison mince
2 tablespoons ready-made caramelized onion
   marmalade
2 teaspoons garlic purée
1 tablespoon finely snipped fresh chives
1 red chilli, deseeded and finely chopped
1 tablespoon olive oil
salt and freshly ground black pepper

1. Remove the skin from the sausages and discard. Put the sausage meat into a large bowl and mix together with the venison, onion marmalade, garlic purée, chives and chilli. Season generously.
2. With wet hands divide the mixture into six portions and shape each one into a patty or burger shape. Put on a baking tray and chill for at least 30 minutes.
3. Heat a griddle pan or barbecue until hot. Lightly brush the burgers with the olive oil and cook on the griddle or barbecue for 5–6 minutes on each side until just cooked. Serve immediately.

## VENISON FILLET
### with Pine Nut Stuffing and Cassis Sauce

Wrap in pancetta to keep the meat succulent and juicy.

**serves 2**

25 g pine nuts, toasted
1 tablespoon olive oil
½ onion, finely chopped
1 tablespoon fresh breadcrumbs
1 tablespoon fresh thyme leaves
2 x 150 g venison leg steaks
4 thin slices of pancetta
30 g clarified butter
50 ml cassis
100 ml beef stock
salt and freshly ground black pepper

1. Whizz half the pine nuts in a small food processor until ground. Set aside. Heat the oil in a frying pan and cook the onion for 3–4 minutes until softened but not browned. Remove from the heat and stir in the ground and whole pine nuts, breadcrumbs and thyme, until combined. Season generously and leave to cool.
2. Preheat the oven to Gas Mark 4/180°C/fan oven 160°C. Put a venison steak on a board and carefully cut a large pocket in the side. Fill with half the stuffing, packing it in. Wrap the steak in two slices of pancetta, making sure the opening is sealed. Repeat with the remaining steak.
3. Melt the butter in an ovenproof frying pan and when starting to sizzle cook the steaks for 4 minutes until brown on both sides. Transfer from the hob to the oven and roast for 5 minutes. Remove the frying pan from the oven. Transfer the venison steaks to a board, cover with foil and leave to rest for 5 minutes.
4. Meanwhile, discard any butter left in the pan. Return the pan to the hob and gently heat. Pour in the cassis and allow it to bubble for 30 seconds. Stir in the stock and bubble for 2–3 minutes until reduced to a light syrup. Season and serve the venison with the cassis sauce.

Other wild meats definitely worth trying are wild boar and rabbit. Both are readily available from good-quality butchers and game suppliers.

## WILD BOAR PIE
### with Apple Pastry Crust

If you can't get hold of wild boar then use pork instead.

**serves 4**

2 tablespoons olive oil
900 g wild boar steaks, cut into chunks
25 g butter
1 red onion, finely chopped
100 g diced pancetta
2 teaspoons dried sage
1 teaspoon dried marjoram
1 tablespoon plain flour
200 ml dry cider
300 ml chicken stock
150 ml double cream
1 egg, beaten
salt and freshly ground black pepper

**for the apple pastry**
125 g plain flour
50 g chilled butter, cubed
1 eating apple, peeled, cored and grated

1. For the apple pastry, put the flour and butter into a food processor and whizz until it resembles fine breadcrumbs. Season with salt and add the grated apple. Pulse until it comes together then empty out on to a clean surface and gently knead until smooth. Wrap in clingfilm and chill in the fridge for at least 30 minutes.

2. Meanwhile heat the oil in a wide lidded pan and cook the wild boar chunks for 5 minutes until browned all over. You will need to do this in batches. Remove and set aside.

3. Add the butter to the pan and gently heat until melted. Stir in the onion, pancetta, sage and marjoram and gently cook for 5–8 minutes, stirring occasionally, until the onion is softened and the pancetta is crispy.

4. Sprinkle over the flour and gently cook for 1 minute, stirring. Then gradually pour in the cider and stock and stir until smooth and combined. Return the meat to the pan and bring to a simmer. Cover and bubble gently for about 1 hour until the boar is tender and the sauce is thickened.

5. Stir in the cream, season generously and bring back to a simmer. Bubble for 10 minutes until thickened then transfer to a 1.5 litre pie dish and leave to cool for 30 minutes.

6. Preheat the oven to Gas Mark 5/190°C/fan oven 170°C. Dust a clean surface with flour and unwrap the pastry. Roll out the pastry until it is 5 mm thick, and then carefully lift on to the pie dish. With a knife, trim the edges and excess pastry. You can use the trimmings to decorate the top. Using your finger and thumb, seal the edges of the pie. Brush the pastry top with beaten egg and bake in the oven for 30–40 minutes until golden and cooked.

# RABBIT RAGU

This delicately flavoured meat is great cooked on or off the bone. Ask your butcher to cut the rabbit into portions for you, and if you prefer it boneless get him to dice the rabbit into small chunks.

serves 4–6

3 tablespoons sunflower oil

900 g rabbit, cut into chunks

1 onion, chopped

2 garlic cloves, crushed

200 g chestnut mushrooms, quartered

50 ml dark rum

1 tablespoon plain flour

3 tablespoons tomato purée

2 tablespoons paprika

2 teaspoons dried chilli flakes

300 ml chicken stock

400 g can chopped tomatoes

salt and freshly ground black pepper

for the topping

2 tablespoons chopped fresh coriander

2 tablespoons chopped fresh parsley

zest of 1 lemon

2 tablespoons jalapeño peppers from a jar, drained and chopped

1. Preheat the oven to Gas Mark 3/160°C/fan oven 140°C. Heat half the oil in a large flameproof casserole pan. Cook the rabbit portions for 5 minutes, turning until brown all over. You will have to do this in batches. Remove and set aside.

2. Add the remaining oil and cook the onion and garlic for 3–4 minutes until softened. Stir in the mushrooms and cook for a further 2 minutes. Pour in the rum and allow it to bubble for a minute. Stir in the flour, tomato purée, paprika and chilli flakes and cook for 1 minute, stirring.

3. Gradually add the chicken stock and stir until combined. Stir in the chopped tomatoes, return the rabbit portions to the pan, season and bring to the boil. Cover and cook in the oven for 1½ hours until the rabbit is tender and the juices have thickened.

4. Meanwhile, in a bowl, mix together all the ingredients for the herb topping. Just before serving, check the seasoning and sprinkle with the herb topping then serve immediately.

# GAME CASSEROLE

**with Herby Dumplings**

You can buy game mix from your butcher and some supermarkets. But if you can't find it, then ask your butcher to make up your own mix. Venison, hare, pheasant, rabbit and guinea fowl all work well.

**serves 4–6**

250 g shallots

2 tablespoons sunflower oil

1 kg game mix, cut into even bite-size chunks

3 streaky bacon rashers, chopped

2 tablespoons plain flour

200 ml white wine

400 ml chicken stock

2 tablespoons white currant or redcurrant jelly

3 fresh rosemary sprigs

salt and freshly ground black pepper

**for the herby dumplings**

50 g suet

100 g self-raising flour

2 tablespoons finely chopped fresh herbs, such as parsley, chives and rosemary

1. Preheat the oven to Gas Mark 3/160°C/fan oven 140°C. Put the shallots into a bowl and cover with boiling water. This makes peeling them a lot easier. Heat the oil in a large flameproof casserole pan. Cook the pieces of game for 5 minutes, turning until brown all over. You will have to do this in batches. Remove and set aside.

2. Drain the shallots and peel, cutting any large ones in half. Return the casserole pan to the heat and cook the shallots and bacon for 5 minutes until starting to brown. Return all the browned game and stir in the flour. Cook for 1 minute, stirring constantly.

3. Gradually pour in the wine and stock and stir until combined. Then add the currant jelly and rosemary. Season and bring to the boil. Cover with a lid, transfer to the oven and cook for 1 hour 15 minutes.

4. After about 1 hour, put all the ingredients for the dumplings into a bowl and season. Add 3–4 tablespoons cold water and stir until it forms a firm but pliable dough. Divide into eight and roll each piece into a small ball. Set aside.

5. Take the casserole from the oven and remove the lid. Sit the dumplings carefully on the surface of the casserole, spaced apart. Return to the oven and bake for a further 45 minutes until the dumplings are golden and the game is tender. Serve immediately.

One thing that stood out to me after rearing and slaughtering livestock was that I didn't want to waste any part of the animal. Offal is the edible internal parts that are removed before the carcass is cut up. For some, the thought of offal is either 'disgusting' or 'old-fashioned'. But for me it truly is heavenly. Not only is it highly nutritious but also it is low in fat and high in iron. I prefer to use lamb's liver and kidney, but you can use calf, pig or chicken livers.

# PAN-FRIED KIDNEYS
## in a Port Sauce

Always cook this dish just before you want to eat – it can't be kept warm as the kidneys will be overcooked. Serve this simple dish with steamed rice.

**serves 4**

450 g lamb's kidneys, prepared and halved (see tip)
1 tablespoon plain flour
30 g clarified butter
1 small onion, finely chopped
75 ml ruby port
2 teaspoons Dijon mustard
200 ml crème fraîche
2 tablespoons finely chopped fresh curly parsley
salt and freshly ground black pepper

1. Dust the kidneys in the flour and shake off the excess. Melt the butter in a pan and cook the onion for 3–4 minutes until softened.
2. Increase the heat and add the kidneys. Pan fry for about 1 minute until the kidneys are browned then pour in the port to deglaze the pan and rapidly bubble for 1 minute until reduced.
3. Stir in the mustard and crème fraîche and continue to bubble for a few more minutes until reduced. Check the seasoning and sprinkle with the parsley. Serve immediately.

**tip** To prepare kidneys, first rinse them in cold water and then pat dry with kitchen paper. Peel away the membrane from each kidney and cut in half. Trim away any gristly core from the centre of each kidney and use as required.

# LIVER AND BACON
**Wild Rocket Salad**

This is a modern-day version of the classic liver and bacon, which, if you've never tried liver before, will soon get your mouth watering.

**serves 2**

about 600 ml sunflower oil for frying

150 g sweet potato, peeled and coarsely grated

30 g butter

1 red onion, thinly sliced

1 teaspoon caster sugar

2 Black Farmer Hickory Smoked Bacon rashers

300 g liver, sliced

1 tablespoon seasoned flour

50 g bag wild rocket

1–2 tablespoons balsamic glaze

salt and freshly ground black pepper

1. Pour sunflower oil into a pan until it is about 2 cm deep. Gently heat for about 5 minutes, or until a cube of bread goes golden brown in 30 seconds. Then fry a spoonful of the grated sweet potato for about 1 minute until golden. Remove with a slotted spoon and drain on kitchen paper. Repeat with the remaining sweet potato. Season the fried sweet potato with salt and set aside. Take the oil off the heat and leave to go cold before discarding.

2. Preheat the grill to medium. Melt half the butter in a frying pan and gently cook the onion and sugar for 8–10 minutes until softened and caramelized, stirring occasionally. Transfer to a bowl. Meanwhile, cook the bacon under the grill for 2–4 minutes until cooked and crispy. Remove and leave to cool, then roughly chop into small pieces.

3. Dust the liver slices in the seasoned flour and shake off the excess. Wipe out the pan used for frying the onion and melt the remaining butter. When melted, fry the liver slices for 1–2 minutes until browned but still a little pink in the middle. You may have to do this in batches. Off the heat, return all the liver and the caramelized onion to the pan, season generously and gently toss to mix.

4. To serve, divide the rocket between two plates and drizzle over the balsamic glaze. Scatter the bacon between the plates and then top each with half the liver and onion. Finish each serving with a handful of the crispy sweet potato shreds and serve immediately.

' Offal is low in fat and high in iron – and highly nutritious! '

Quite rightly there has been a lot of outrage over the years about how calves for veal have been reared and whether it is ethical or not to enjoy this meat. But one way to avoid this is to make sure you buy organic British veal, commonly known as rose veal, from good-quality butchers or suppliers. The meat is darker pink and very flavoursome with little fat, due to the young age of the calf, and is just as versatile as chicken.

## ZURICH-STYLE VEAL

If you don't want to use veal then you can substitute skinless chicken breast fillets or pork escalopes instead. Serve with fried potato rosti and a generous green salad.

**serves 4**

30 g clarified butter
2 x 175 g veal escalopes, each cut into 4 pieces
100 g lamb's kidneys, prepared and chopped
2 shallots, finely chopped
150 g baby button mushrooms, trimmed
75 ml gin
300 ml single cream
1 chicken stock cube
½ teaspoon dried thyme
salt and white pepper

1. Gently heat half the butter in a wide frying pan and brown the veal and kidneys for 2–3 minutes. You will need to do this in batches. Remove and set aside.
2. Melt the remaining butter in the same pan and cook the shallots for 2–3 minutes until softened. Add the mushrooms and continue to cook for 5 minutes. Pour in the gin and rapidly bubble for 1 minute until almost evaporated.
3. Stir in the cream, crumbled stock cube and thyme, and return the veal and kidney. Gently bring to a simmer for 1–2 minutes, or until the sauce is thickened and the veal is cooked. Season with salt and white pepper and serve immediately.

## OSSO BUCCO

**serves 4**

2 tablespoons olive oil
4 veal shins or osso bucco
1 onion, finely chopped
2 carrots, finely diced
1 celery stick, finely diced
4 garlic cloves, peeled
1 tablespoon plain flour
250 ml red wine
250 ml beef stock
1 tablespoon caster sugar
2 x 400 g cans chopped tomatoes
4 bay leaves
1 tablespoon mixed dried Italian herbs
salt and freshly ground black pepper

1. Preheat the oven to Gas Mark 4/180°C/fan oven 160°C. Heat the oil in a large flameproof casserole pan and cook the veal shins for 5 minutes, turning until brown all over. Remove and set aside. You may need to do this in batches. Add the onion, carrot, celery and garlic to the pan and cook for 8–10 minutes until softened and golden.
2. Sprinkle over the flour and cook for 1 minute, stirring. Gradually pour in the red wine and beef stock and stir until smooth and combined. Add the caster sugar, tomatoes, bay leaves and dried herbs and return the veal shins to the pan. Season generously and bring to the boil.
3. Cover and cook in the oven for 2 hours or until the veal is tender and the sauce is thickened. Check the seasoning and serve immediately.

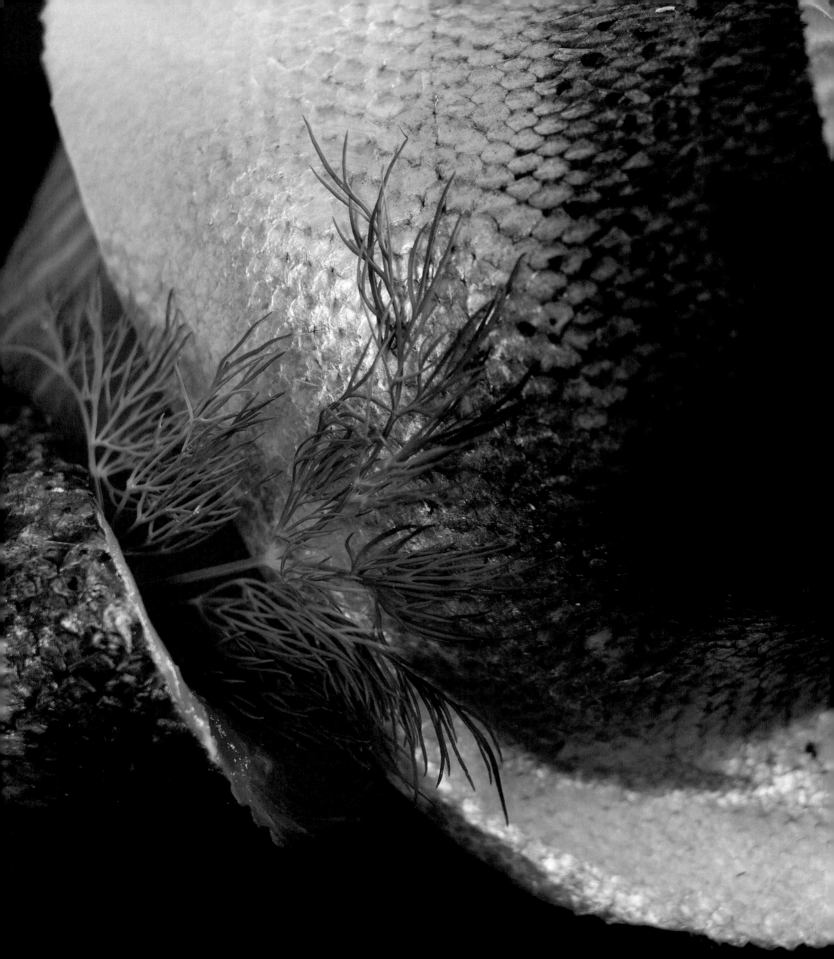

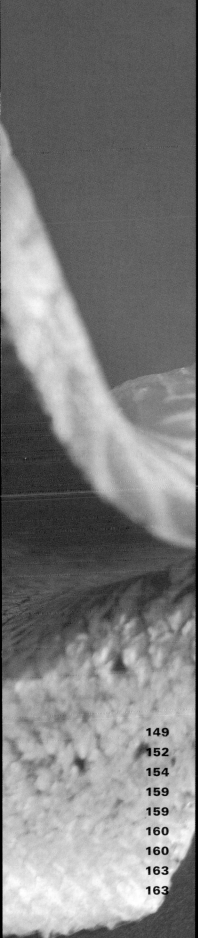

FISH

I bought my farm in the autumn of 1999. The previous owner was a dairy farmer and, like him, many dairy farmers of that time were struggling to make farming work for them. I may have achieved my lifelong ambition to own a farm but to bring the place up to modern-day standards was going to bleed nearly every last penny out of me. The farm had a large farmhouse and three substantial traditional stone barns that had been used for housing animals. All of the buildings were in urgent need of repair. There was no mains water to the farm – it had to be manually pumped daily into the house. No gas, no central heating. Everything was in a sorry state. There was nothing for it but to rebuild the house from top to bottom. This had not been my original plan when I bought it, so I had to scrape together all the money I could find to undertake the building works. Having done up a couple of properties previously I knew that the rule of thumb is to make sure that you are on the job every single day to manage the project. There is nothing like haemorrhaging money to focus the mind and to get the build finished on time. With all the work going on in the house I had to find somewhere to stay. As I searched around, one place kept being recommended. Little did I know then that this establishment was to play a major part in my life and also rekindle a love of fish.

The Arundell Arms in Lifton, Devon, became my home from home for many months while I was rebuilding my farmhouse. Every night I would return to this understated quaint inn and, the moment I stepped through the door, all the troubles of the day would wash away. Each evening I would be greeted with kind words of encouragement from the owner, Anne Voss-Bark.

The Arundell Arms is one of those places that is very comfortable in its own skin and has not been seduced by the modern trappings of small country hotels. The place is full of history and nostalgia. The pictures on the walls are not a job-lot imported from the East. Each one tells part of a story – as though you had been let into a private world. Going back there every night was like returning to the home of a favourite aunt. Anne Voss-Bark is friendly but not prying. She is the template of what good old-fashioned hospitality can be like at its best. It is the sort of rural hotel that gives you an idea of how England used to be some fifty years ago. Everyone is welcome, including children and dogs – a rarity these days. All that is expected in return is that you abide by the rules of rural living – courtesy and respect.

Usually when I stay in a hotel I tend to order a steak or burger. I work on the principle that most things that are cooked in the kitchen will be cooked from frozen and the chef's skills will leave a lot to be desired, so I go for the dish with least risk. Sitting in the restaurant on the first night of my stay I scanned the menu, looking for some simple fare to order. I was disappointed that my staples were not on the menu and I searched in desperation to find something familiar. I became fraught as the menu was dominated with fish dishes, and in my rulebook fish was certainly a no-no. When I was a child a fish bone got stuck in my throat and, as a result, I had a pathological fear of it happening again. From that day I had hardly ever eaten fish. After a hard day's work I was hungry and I was at a loss as to what to do. The waiter could sense my mounting anguish and intervened. 'You must try the Five Fishes, it's to die for.' Dying was what I was afraid of. 'Haven't you got any steak?' 'No,' came the reply, 'but do try the Five Fishes. If you don't like it I won't charge you for it.'

When the dish arrived it looked lovely, but it was going to take more than good looks to seduce me. I cautiously took my first bite and I was hooked. My taste buds had fallen head over heels in love, so much so that for the next ten nights I wouldn't eat anything else.

This recipe is dedicated to the Arundell Arms. I also have to thank them for getting me to enjoy fish again and over the period of my stay I enjoyed a number of fish dishes. Without them this chapter would not have appeared in this book.

## FIVE FISHES

It is really up to you what fish you use in this dish – if you want you can just use salmon or cod. That's the great thing about cooking, you really are the boss, so don't be afraid to experiment.

**serves 4**

vegetable oil for deep frying
150 g plain flour or '00' flour
250 ml ice-cold sparkling water
125 g skinless salmon fillet, cut into 4 chunks
125 g skinless trout fillet, cut into 4 chunks
125 g skinless cod loin, cut into 4 chunks or goujons
125 g skinless haddock loin, cut into 4 chunks or goujons
125 g tuna steak, cut into 4 goujons
lemon wedges to serve
salt and freshly ground black pepper

**for the herby mayonnaise**
6 tablespoons mayonnaise
1 garlic clove, crushed
3 tablespoons mixed chopped fresh herbs, such as chives, parsley and dill
zest of 1 lemon

1. Make the mayonnaise by mixing together all the ingredients in a small bowl. Season generously and chill until needed.

2. Heat a deep-fat fryer or put the oil in a large pan and heat to 180°C. This is when a cube of bread will turn golden within 60 seconds. Meanwhile, put the flour and plenty of seasoning into a large bowl and place over a bowl of ice. This helps to keep the batter cold. Slowly pour in the sparkling water and stir with a fork. Don't overwork the mixture, it doesn't matter if there are lumps.

3. Once the oil has reached the correct temperature, using a slotted spoon, coat a piece of salmon in the batter and then deep fry for 3–5 minutes (depending on the thickness) until cooked and deep golden brown. Drain on kitchen paper and season with salt. Keep warm in the oven while you coat and fry the remaining fish.

4. Serve the fish warm with the herby mayonnaise and lemon wedges.

The location of the Arundell Arms has a lot to do with the real love of fish there. The hotel sits on the River Tamar and it owns fishing rights along the river. Adorning the walls of the bar and reception areas are pictures of fishermen showing off their catches. These are pictures of a bygone age. Fishing rods had pride of place and the different flies used for fly-fishing were put into frames that are usually reserved for pictures of loved ones.

People from all over the country come to this hotel to learn and master the art of fly-fishing, and such is their passion for fish they convinced me to give fly-fishing a try. Now they may have got me to enjoy eating fish again but I didn't think I had the temperament to be a fisherman. I am a man who wants instant results, and the idea of spending hours on the river bank patiently casting a line to catch a fish didn't seem to fit. But such is the power of people's enthusiasm I was convinced to give it a go.

If you want to learn how to fly-fish I can't recommend this place highly enough. There are two ghillies who patiently take the beginner through the basics. The hotel is blessed with a well-stocked lake, which is an ideal location for the beginner to learn. I remember well when I caught my first trout, and in particular the moment the fish took the bait. At that moment I understood why so many people enjoy the sport of fly-fishing. Unlike the other main ingredients in this book, fish is the only one that can go from source to plate in a matter of minutes. There was going to be only one dish on the night's menu: Baked Trout in a Salt Crust.

# BAKED TROUT IN A SALT CRUST

Don't be thinking that all this salt will make the trout taste too salty. In fact it doesn't taste salty at all, just perfectly seasoned. The salt dough simply produces a deliciously succulent and juicy fish. If you can't find smoked salt then use regular flaked salt.

**serves 4**

2 whole trout (about 350 g each), gutted and cleaned
2 lemongrass sticks, outer leaves removed and
    sticks halved lengthways
a small handful of fresh chives
a small handful of fresh thyme
3 garlic cloves, halved
1 lemon, cut into slices
freshly ground black pepper

**for the salt crust**
550 g plain flour
250 g smoked flaked sea salt
2 eggs, beaten

1. Preheat the oven to Gas Mark 7/220°C/fan oven 200°C. To make the salt crust, put the flour and salt in a bowl. Make a well in the centre and pour in the beaten eggs. Gently mix to combine, gradually adding about 200 ml cold water until the mixture becomes a firm dough.

2. Divide the dough in half and roll one half on a large piece of parchment paper until it is about the thickness of a £1 coin and a large oblong, as long as the trout.

3. Put a whole trout into the centre of the oblong and season the cavity with black pepper. Stuff the cavity with half the lemongrass, chives, thyme, garlic and lemon slices. Brush the exposed dough with cold water and then carefully fold the dough up and over the trout to enclose the fish completely. Mould the dough around the trout, sealing the edges and making sure there are no air gaps. Trim away any excess dough. Repeat with the remaining dough and trout.

4. Transfer the trout parcels to a large non-stick baking tray and bake in the oven for 20 minutes or until the crust is light golden. Remove from the oven and set aside for 10 minutes.

5. To serve: using a sharp knife or pair of scissors cut off the top half of the salt crust from each baked trout and discard. Carefully lift off the top fillet and transfer to a serving plate. Discard the head and back bone to reveal the bottom fillet. Carefully remove this fillet and set aside with the other fillets. Serve immediately.

' As I tucked into this dish I felt the same sense of achievement and satisfaction as I did when I ate the first lamb that I reared. '

There is only one other person who can prepare fish to the standard of the Arundell Arms' chef and that's Michaela, my wife. As a family, when we want a special treat we all ask in unison for her fish pie. When Michaela makes it the day starts early for her because there is only one place that she trusts to get the fish and that's a small village shop at Widemouth Bay just outside Bude on the North Cornwall coast. I am sure this shop must have a name, but with it being the only shop in Widemouth Bay I have never thought it important to remember it. This shop sells everything and at first glance the impression is that it is just a classic convenience store, but it is worth your while looking at the fish counter, for there you will find an assortment of delicious freshly caught fish.

## MICHAELA'S FISH PIE
**with Saffron Mash**

You don't have to use quails' eggs but I like the richness they add to this dish.

**serves 4**

8 quails' eggs
175 g raw shelled tiger prawns
250 g skinless cod or haddock loin, cut into chunks
250 g skinless lightly smoked salmon fillet, cut
   into chunks
salt and freshly ground black pepper

**for the saffron mash**
900 g floury potatoes, peeled and cut into chunks
4 tablespoons full fat milk
25 g butter
2 large pinches of saffron, lightly crushed

**for the sauce**
50 g butter
25 g plain flour
500 ml creamy Jersey milk
2 tablespoons chopped fresh dill
2 tablespoons chopped fresh parsley
½ tablespoon capers, rinsed and finely chopped

1. Put the quails' eggs into a pan of boiling water for 2–3 minutes. Drain and plunge into cold water, then peel and set aside.

2. For the mash, put the potatoes into a large pan of cold salted water and bring to the boil. Simmer gently for 20 minutes until tender. Meanwhile, gently heat the milk and butter in a small pan until simmering. Take off the heat and stir in the saffron. Leave to infuse. Drain the potatoes and return to the pan.

3. For the sauce, melt the butter in a saucepan, stir in the flour and cook for 1 minute, stirring, until foamy. Remove from the heat and then very gradually whisk in the milk until smooth and combined. Stir in the dill, parsley and capers and season generously. Set aside.

4. Preheat the oven to Gas Mark 6/200°C/fan oven 180°C. Mash the potato with a potato ricer (or masher) until smooth. Stir in the saffron milk and seasoning and set aside.

5. Arrange the prawns and chunks of fish over the base of a 1.5 litre ovenproof dish. Top with the peeled quails' eggs, well spaced apart, and then pour over the herby white sauce. Pipe or spoon the mashed potato over the top, swirling with the back of a spoon. Bake in the oven for 25 minutes until golden and bubbling. Leave to stand for 5–10 minutes before serving.

# RED SNAPPER CEVICHE

The acid from the lime will cure the fish and turn it opaque. If you prefer your fish 'cooked' a little more, leave it a bit longer. Serve with warmed ciabatta to dip in the juices.

**serves 2**

300 g skinless red snapper fillets
zest and juice of 3 limes
1 red chilli, deseeded and finely diced
3 tablespoons extra virgin olive oil
½ red onion, finely chopped
2 tablespoons chopped fresh coriander
50 g wild rocket
1 chicory bulb, finely sliced
¼ cucumber, deseeded and diced
75 g cherry tomatoes, halved
salt and freshly ground black pepper

1. Cut the red snapper into thin strips, about 1 cm in width, and place in a large bowl. Add the lime zest and juice, chilli, extra virgin olive oil and onion. Stir to combine and then set aside for at least 30 minutes.

2. Add the coriander, rocket, chicory, cucumber and cherry tomatoes to the red snapper mixture and toss to coat. Season generously and divide between two plates. Drizzle with any remaining dressing and serve.

# JAMAICAN SALT FISH FRITTERS

If you can't find salt cod then use the same quantity of cod fillets, but there is no need to soak the cod for 12 hours so start the recipe from step 2.

**serves 6**

400 g salt cod
5 spring onions, finely chopped
1 green pepper, deseeded and finely diced
2 garlic cloves, crushed
1 scotch bonnet chilli, deseeded and finely diced
125 g self-raising flour
1 teaspoon dried fast-action yeast
150 ml warm full fat milk
about 1 litre vegetable oil for deep frying
freshly ground black pepper

1. Put the salt cod into a large bowl of water and chill for 12 hours, rinsing the cod and changing the water every 4 hours.

2. Drain and rinse the cod and put into a wide lidded saucepan. Cover with water and bring to the boil. Take off the heat, cover and leave for 10–15 minutes or until the fish flakes. Meanwhile, put the spring onions, green pepper, garlic and chilli into a large bowl. Put the flour and yeast into another large bowl. Gradually whisk in the warm milk until smooth and season generously with black pepper. Set aside.

3. Drain the cod then carefully remove the skin and any bones. Flake the cod into large pieces and put into the bowl with the spring onions. Pour in the batter and then mix to combine thoroughly.

4. Heat a deep-fat fryer or put the oil in a large saucepan until it reaches 180°C. Carefully lower a generous heaped tablespoon of the cod mixture into the hot oil and cook for 3–5 minutes until golden and cooked. Remove with a slotted spoon and drain on kitchen paper. Keep warm in the oven and cook the remaining mixture in batches. Serve immediately.

# CRISPY FISH AND CHIPS

You will never go to a chip shop again after this.

serves 4

250 g plain flour
7 g sachet dried yeast
330 ml bottle Mexican beer
900 g floury potatoes, peeled and cut into 1 cm thick
    chips
about 2 litres vegetable oil for deep frying
4 x 200 g mahi mahi fillets
salt
malt vinegar, lemon wedges and tartar sauce,
    to serve

1. Put the flour, yeast and a pinch of salt into a bowl. Gradually add the beer and gently whisk until smooth. Leave in a warm place for an hour, or until tiny bubbles appear on the surface and your chips are cooked.
2. Meanwhile, put the chips into a pan of cold salted water and bring to the boil. Simmer very gently for 2–3 minutes then carefully drain and dry with kitchen paper. Heat a deep-fat fryer or put the oil in a large pan and gently heat to 130°C. Cook the chips for 5 minutes until very light golden. Drain on kitchen paper and set aside to cool.
3. Preheat the oven to Gas Mark 3/160°C/fan oven 140°C. Increase the heat in the fryer or pan to 190°C and cook the chips again for 2–3 minutes until dark golden and crispy. Drain on kitchen paper and sprinkle with salt. You will have to do this in batches. Keep the first batch warm in the oven while you cook the remaining chips.
4. When all the chips are cooked increase the temperature of the oil to 220°C. Then carefully dip one mahi mahi fillet in the batter until coated and place in the hot oil, lowering the fish away from you. Cook the fish for 2–4 minutes until golden and crispy and the fish is cooked. Drain on kitchen paper and keep warm in the oven. You will have to do this in batches.
5. When all the fish is cooked, serve the chips and fish immediately with lemon juice, tartar sauce and malt vinegar.

# PRAWNS IN SPICY COCONUT SAUCE

This is a perfect light meal for four when served with steamed jasmine rice.

serves 4

2 teaspoons hot paprika
2 teaspoons mild or medium curry powder
½ teaspoon celery salt
½ teaspoon garlic granules
½ teaspoon dried thyme
¼ teaspoon ground cinnamon
400 g large raw tiger prawns, shelled
juice of 1 lemon plus lemon wedges to serve
1 tablespoon olive oil
1 small onion, finely chopped
1 small hot green chilli, finely chopped
1 tablespoon tomato purée
½ teaspoon shrimp paste
400 ml can coconut milk
2 tablespoons chopped fresh coriander
freshly ground black pepper

1. Put the paprika, curry powder, celery salt, garlic granules, thyme and cinnamon into a large freezer bag and shake to combine, holding the top closed. Add the prawns and the lemon juice and seal the bag. Massage the prawns from the outside to coat in the spices. Set aside.
2. Heat the oil in a wide, deep frying pan and gently cook the onion and chilli for 5–8 minutes until soft but not coloured. Add the tomato purée and shrimp paste and cook for 1 minute, stirring.
3. Empty the prawns and spices from the freezer bag into the pan and cook for a further minute, stirring. Pour in the coconut milk and gently bring just to the boil. Reduce the heat and simmer for 2–3 minutes until the prawns are cooked and the coconut milk has thickened. Season generously with black pepper and serve immediately, sprinkled with the coriander and with lemon wedges.

# CLAM CHOWDER

This thick creamy soup is delicious served with crusty bread
to mop up the last remaining dregs in the bowl.

serves 4

500 g fresh clams in their shells, cleaned

150 ml dry white wine

100 ml fish stock

50 g butter

1 onion, chopped

3 Black Farmer Hickory Smoked Bacon rashers,
    chopped

2 tablespoons plain flour

1 tablespoon Cajun spices

750 ml full fat milk

2 potatoes, peeled and diced

1 tablespoon finely snipped fresh chives

salt and freshly ground black pepper

1 Discard any open clams that don't close when gently
tapped on a board. Put the clams, white wine and fish stock
into a large lidded saucepan and bring to the boil. Cover and
simmer for 5–8 minutes, shaking the pan occasionally until
the shells open. Drain the clams, reserving the cooking liquid
in a jug. Discard any clams that have not opened. Remove
the clams from their shells and set aside.

2. Melt the butter in a large saucepan and cook the onion and
bacon gently for 3–4 minutes until the onion has softened
but not browned. Stir in the flour and Cajun spices and cook
for 1 minute, stirring. Gradually stir in the milk until smooth
and combined. Season generously.

3. Pass the reserved clam cooking liquid through a sieve into
the pan. Then stir in the potatoes and bring to the boil. Gently
simmer for 15 minutes.

4. Stir in the cooked clams and gently cook for 5 minutes until
the potatoes are tender. Ladle into bowls, check seasoning
and sprinkle with the chives.

# SALMON STEAKS

### with Lime and Ginger Sauce

serves 4

4 x 175 g salmon fillets with skin on

1 tablespoon olive oil

for the lime and ginger sauce

50 ml sunflower oil

1 small onion, finely chopped

1 tablespoon garlic purée

50 g tomato purée

1 teaspoon hot paprika

1½ tablespoons ground ginger

75 g clear honey

zest and juice of 3 limes

1 vegetable stock cube

100 ml water

salt and freshly ground black pepper

1. Heat half the sunflower oil in a small frying pan and cook
the onion for 3–4 minutes until soft. Leave to cool. Transfer
to a small food processor and add the remaining sunflower
oil and garlic and tomato purées. Whizz until puréed. Add the
remaining sauce ingredients and whizz until smooth.

2. With a sharp knife make three or four small deep slits
through the skin of the salmon fillets. Put the fish into a
non-metallic dish and spoon over half the lime and ginger
sauce, turning to coat. Leave to marinate for about 1 hour.

3. Heat the olive oil in a heavy non-stick frying pan. Remove
the salmon from the marinade, wiping off any excess.
Discard the marinade. Gently cook the salmon, skin side
down, for about 4–5 minutes, or until the skin releases easily
from the pan. Flip over and cook for a further 2–3 minutes,
making sure that you don't overcook the fish. Leave in the
pan and loosely cover with foil.

4. Meanwhile, gently heat the remaining sauce in a small pan
and adjust the seasoning. When the fish is cooked arrange it
on four plates and drizzle with the hot lime and ginger sauce.
Serve immediately.

# PORK

We sat there in silence. Not the easy silence of being at one with each other, but the sort of silence that was heavy with tension. As the minutes ticked away, the tension kept building. I had long ago given up shouting and screaming, all that was left now was to leave my future to Fate. Being a man unused to leaving things to Fate, this uncomfortable silence was the only way I could think to manage the situation. I was in the confined space of a transit van with my travelling colleague, a bubbly Australian who I nicknamed 'No Worries' because whatever life chucked at him he would always bounce back with a charming 'no worries, mate'. But today even he knew better than to come out with his pet phrase.

The previous evening we had loaded the vehicle with all the equipment we needed to run a small mobile kitchen. We were travelling abroad, and my previous experiences travelling overseas had taught me that anyone doing anything slightly unusual could find themselves stuck at the border while officialdom takes its painfully slow course in sorting out access, especially if amongst your cargo are things like large gas bottles.

Today's journey was very important and I had put a lot of effort into making sure that everything would run smoothly, but it was beginning to look as if I was going to fall at the final hurdle. It wouldn't be worth going if I didn't get delivery of the precious cargo that was currently holding up proceedings. Some weeks previously I had been asked if I would be interested in going on a food mission to a French market with a selected group of south-west food producers, to show the French the very best West Country food products. For years I have been frustrated that we British always seem to flock to French markets when they come here, but we don't have the equivalent British markets for the French. We produce some excellent foods in this country, not least in the West Country, and what we need to do is shout about it – here and abroad. I am very proud to be British and I had planned a grand arrival on French soil. I was armed with a huge Union Jack and I had had the flag of Devon specially made up for the trip. Once on French soil I was going to march in front of my transit van flying the flags with the words 'The Black Farmer – Flavours without Frontiers' emblazoned across my chest.

Sitting in that transit van being toyed with by the gods was a million miles away from my grand entrance. What lay ahead now was disaster and my reputation in tatters. The reason I had been asked on this trip was because my sausages have consistently won awards. (In fact, as I write this book in August 2008, I have just been informed that they have won a Gold Great Taste Award, an accolade I shall cherish because these are the 'Oscars' of the food industry.) I have been campaigning for years to get butchers and sausage producers to put more quality meat into sausages and not stuff them with too much breadcrumb. Traditionally butchers put the fag ends of the pig into sausages, mixed with liberal quantities of fat and breadcrumbs. As a consequence many people have been put off eating them because, quite frankly, they tasted awful. In fact it was my disappointment with the quality of the sausages on the market that led me to create my own.

I am very proud of my sausages, which have a very high meat content, made from pork shoulder and belly, and are gluten free and I am prepared to travel the world evangelizing about them, but to be able to do this you need to have the product in the first place. The reason for my angst that day was that my sausages had not arrived and I had got only two hours to reach the ferry. I had been promised that my products would arrive before nine and this courier company had never let me down yet, but with the clock pointing to 8.55 it looked as if today they were going to.

There was no point asking 'No Worries' the time, for I knew the truth of the situation and just had to accept it – it was 9.15, the courier had not turned up with my sausages, and I would have to ring the group I was travelling with to tell them that I wouldn't be making it. I was deeply disappointed and was bursting to take my anger out on someone or something. I hate failure, especially when it is due to incompetence. I have always believed that when you are planning any event you should anticipate the cock-ups and I was kicking myself for not going with my instinct to have had my sausages delivered the day before. My rationale for getting them delivered that morning was that I wanted them freshly made.

As I started to dial, an incoming call got there first: 'Where are you, mate? I've busted a gut to get here and I can't see you anywhere.' 'Who am I speaking to?' 'The courier.' It was as though the gods had heard my plea for someone to take my anger and frustration out on, and who better than the hapless courier? I do anger very well but I knew this was going to be one of my best performances ever. 'Are you having a fxxxing laugh? I am sitting outside the lane of my farm and I can't see you, and from where I am I can see everything for miles.' 'What farm? I'm at the ferry port. You said you were catching the 9 a.m. ferry.'

I could go on and explain how and why the instructions got mixed up, but at this point I was so relieved, I just wanted to get to the port, because now I knew that I would make it. I turned to 'No Worries' and told him to get driving. He gave me one of his wry cheeky smiles and said, 'No worries, mate.'

It's funny how extremely stressful situations can push creativity to the fore. I can remember what food dishes were going through my mind on that dreadful day, and I'd like to share some of them with you now as they are really delicious.

After our shaky start we arrived in France safely and triumphed at the British food market. I had a fantastic day introducing my sausages to the French and I even had the opportunity to march through the market waving my flags. Really surprising to me was how unfamiliar the French were with the British sausage and how to cook it. There is no greater sense of pride than teaching the French something about food!

# CAJUN PORK

This hot and spicy stew is perfectly warming but if you like it a bit more fiery you can keep the seeds in the chillies.

serves 4-6

1.25 kg boneless pork shoulder joint, excess fat trimmed and cut into 2.5 cm cubes
4 green chillies, deseeded and chopped
3 garlic cloves, chopped
1 teaspoon cayenne pepper
2 tablespoons Cajun seasoning
2 tablespoons olive oil
1 large onion, chopped
1 red pepper, deseeded and chopped into large pieces
1 yellow pepper, deseeded and chopped into large pieces
1 tablespoon plain flour
300 ml chicken stock
100 ml red wine
400 g can chopped tomatoes
2 tablespoons light muscovado sugar
a small handful of fresh thyme
salt and freshly ground black pepper

1. Put the pork into a large non-metallic bowl and add the chillies, garlic, cayenne and Cajun seasoning. Mix together to coat and set aside for 1 hour.

2. Heat the oil in a heavy-based flameproof casserole pan and cook the pork cubes for 5 minutes until browned all over. You may need to do this in batches. Remove and set aside. Add the onion and cook for 3–4 minutes, then stir in the peppers and cook for a further 3–4 minutes until starting to soften and brown. Return the pork to the pan and sprinkle over the flour. Cook for 1 minute then gradually add the chicken stock, stirring until combined. Pour in the red wine and stir in the chopped tomatoes, sugar and thyme. Bring to the boil then cover and simmer for 2 hours until the pork is tender. Check the seasoning and serve immediately.

# LEMON AND WILD MYRTLE PORK ESCALOPES

Myrtle leaves are available dried and can be found in the herbs and spices section of large supermarkets. They give a subtle aroma of eucalyptus.

serves 4

3 heaped tablespoons dried wild myrtle leaves
3 tablespoons olive oil
½ teaspoon Dijon mustard
zest and juice of ½ lemon
4 pork escalopes
salt and freshly ground black pepper

1. Put the myrtle leaves into a mortar and pestle and crush. Place in a large freezer bag along with the olive oil, mustard and lemon zest and juice. Season generously. Add the pork escalopes, seal the bag and massage the marinade into the pork. Leave to marinate in the fridge for 1 hour or up to 8 hours.

2. Preheat the barbecue or a griddle until hot. Remove the pork escalopes from the freezer bag and discard the marinade. Cook the escalopes for 5–8 minutes, turning halfway through, until the pork is cooked. Leave the pork to rest for 5 minutes covered with foil before serving.

# STICKY PORK CHOPS

The muscovado sauce is infused with Chinese five spice, a blend of spices including ginger, fennel, cloves and star anise.
**serves 6**

2 tablespoons olive oil
6 pork loin chops

**for the muscovado sauce**
1 tablespoon olive oil
1 onion, finely chopped
1 teaspoon garlic purée
2 teaspoons tomato purée
1 red chilli, finely chopped
200 g can chopped tomatoes
100 g dark muscovado sugar
2 teaspoons Chinese five-spice powder
3 tablespoons light soy sauce
75 ml red wine
1 vegetable stock cube
1 teaspoon balsamic vinegar

1. To make the sauce, heat the oil in a wide pan and cook the onion for 3–4 minutes until starting to soften. Add the garlic and tomato purées and cook for 1 minute. Stir in all the remaining ingredients and gently heat, stirring occasionally until the sugar has dissolved. Bring to a simmer and gently bubble for 20 minutes.

2. Meanwhile, heat 2 tablespoons olive oil in a frying pan and cook the pork chops for 5 minutes until browned all over. You will have to do this in batches. Transfer the chops to the sauce and simmer gently for 5–8 minutes until the pork is cooked and the sauce is reduced and thickened. Serve immediately.

# EVER SO STICKY RIBS

Adults and kids will love eating these, just make sure you have enough wet wipes for when you've finished.
**serves 4**

150 g black cherry jam
100 ml ketchup
50 ml red wine vinegar
50 ml Worcestershire sauce
1 tablespoon dried chilli flakes
3 tablespoons sunflower oil
1.25 kg pork belly ribs
salt

1. Pass the black cherry jam through a sieve into a large bowl, pressing it through with the back of a spoon. Add the ketchup, red wine vinegar, Worcestershire sauce, chilli flakes and oil. Mix everything together and season with a little salt.

2. Add the pork belly ribs and toss to coat in the jammy mixture. Tip into a non-stick roasting tin and pour over any leftover mixture. Leave to marinate for at least 1 hour or up to 4 hours in the fridge.

3. Preheat the oven to Gas Mark 4/180°C/fan oven 160°C. Cover the roasting tin with foil and bake the ribs for 1½ hours in the oven. Remove the foil and continue to cook for a further 45 minutes until the ribs are starting to char and caramelize and the meat falls off the bone. Leave to cool slightly before serving.

## PIGS IN BLANKET PIE

Succulent sausages wrapped with bacon hidden under a golden crust. Serve with a selection of green vegetables.

**serves 4**

8 streaky bacon rashers
8 Black Farmer Premium pork sausages
2 tablespoons olive oil
1 large onion, finely sliced
1 tablespoon plain flour
300 ml chicken stock
150 ml dry white wine
1 tablespoon whole grain mustard
375 g pack ready-rolled shortcrust pastry
1 egg, beaten
salt and freshly ground black pepper

1. Using the back of a knife, carefully stretch each rasher of bacon slightly. Wrap a rasher of bacon around each sausage. Heat 1 tablespoon oil in a large non-stick frying pan and cook the sausages, bacon seam side down first, for 5 minutes, turning until lightly brown all over. You may need to do this in batches. Remove and put into a 1.5 litre pie dish.

2. Heat the remaining oil in the frying pan and gently cook the onion for 5–8 minutes until softened but not coloured. Add the flour and cook for 1 minute, stirring. Gradually stir in the chicken stock until combined, then add the white wine and bring to the boil, stirring until thickened. Stir in the mustard and check the seasoning. Pour into the pie dish and leave to cool for 30 minutes.

3. Preheat the oven to Gas Mark 5/190°C/fan oven 170°C. Unroll the pastry and carefully lift on to the pie dish. With a knife, carefully trim the edges and excess pastry. You can use the trimmings to decorate the top. Using your finger and thumb, seal the edges of the pie. Brush the pastry top with beaten egg and bake in the oven for 30–40 minutes until golden and cooked.

## THE BLACK FARMER CASSOULET

This French-inspired peasant dish is the perfect winter warmer.

**serves 6–8**

2 tablespoons sunflower oil
6 Black Farmer Premium pork sausages, halved
500 g thick belly pork rashers, cut into small chunks
2 onions, cut into wedges
2 garlic cloves, crushed
2 tablespoons tomato purée
1 tablespoon black treacle
2 teaspoons golden syrup
2 teaspoons mustard powder
50 g dark muscovado sugar
1 tablespoon dried oregano
400 g can chopped tomatoes
450 ml chicken stock
2 x 410 g cans cannellini beans
25 g fresh breadcrumbs
2 tablespoons chopped fresh oregano

1. Preheat the oven to Gas Mark 3/160°C/fan oven 140°C. Heat half the oil in a flameproof casserole pan and cook the sausages and belly pork for 5 minutes until brown all over. You will need to do this in batches. Remove and set aside.

2. Add the onions and garlic to the pan with the remaining oil and cook for a further 5 minutes until softened and starting to brown. Stir in the tomato purée, treacle, golden syrup, mustard powder, sugar and dried oregano and gently heat until the sugar has dissolved.

3. Stir in the chopped tomatoes, stock and cannellini beans and return the sausages and pork to the pan. Bring to the boil, cover and cook in the oven for 1½ hours.

4. Remove the casserole from the oven and remove the lid. Sprinkle over the breadcrumbs and oregano and return to the oven for 15–20 minutes or until the crumbs are golden brown. Serve immediately.

# MILK-BRAISED PORK LOIN
## with Chilli Crackling

The idea of cooking the pork in milk is Italian inspired, and helps this lean cut stay juicy. But nothing is wasted as the cooking liquor is used to make the sauce. Serve with gnocchi to soak up the juices.

**serves 6**

1.25 kg rolled pork loin or boneless leg of pork
2 garlic cloves, peeled
4 whole cloves
a small handful of fresh thyme
1.2 litres full fat milk
2 tablespoons sunflower oil
1–2 teaspoons dried chilli flakes
1 tablespoon cornflour
4 tablespoons crème fraîche
salt and freshly ground black pepper

1. Preheat the oven to Gas Mark 2/150°C/fan oven 130°C. Cut the string from around the pork, then carefully cut off the skin in one piece leaving a thin layer of fat on the meat. Re-tie the pork in four or five places. Heat a flameproof casserole pan, one that the pork will fit into snugly, and cook the meat for 5 minutes, turning until browned all over.

2. Remove from the heat and put the garlic, cloves and thyme under the pork joint in the casserole dish. Pour over the milk, return to the heat and gently bring to the boil – don't worry if the milk curdles. Meanwhile, to make the chilli crackling, score the pork skin in a criss-cross pattern. Rub the oil into the skin and then rub in the dried chilli and lots of salt. Place in a roasting tin and put in the oven on the bottom shelf.

3. When the pork has come to the boil, transfer the casserole dish to the oven, on the shelf above the crackling and cook for 1½ hours until the pork is cooked, basting the meat occasionally.

4. Remove the casserole from the oven and set aside. Increase the oven temperature to Gas Mark 7/220°C/fan oven 200°C and put the crackling on a higher shelf. Cook for 30 minutes or until golden and crispy. Meanwhile, carefully remove the pork from the milky cooking liquor and transfer to a board. Loosely cover with foil and set aside.

5. Carefully pass the milky liquor through a sieve into a jug. You should be left with about 400 ml. Put the cornflour in a small pan and then add 1–2 tablespoons cooking liquor and stir to dissolve. Gradually stir in the rest of the liquor and the crème fraîche until smooth. Gently bring to a simmer for 1–2 minutes until thickened. Check the seasoning and keep warm until the crackling is ready.

6. To serve, carve the pork into thick slices and break up the crackling into chunks. Serve the pork with the cream sauce and crackling.

Sausages are the soul of The Black Farmer brand and I believe a great-tasting sausage can be the basis for many a meal. Although sausage and mash with onion gravy is the ultimate comfort food, the following sausage recipes will hopefully inspire you to expand your repertoire and relive the wonders of the sausage!

## SAUSAGES WITH SPICY TOMATO LENTILS

This hearty dish is a great way to enjoy the humble sausage.

**serves 6**

250 g Puy lentils
1 tablespoon olive oil
2 x 400 g packs Black Farmer sausages
2 red onions, sliced
3 garlic cloves, crushed
2 large carrots, diced
1 large rosemary sprig
600 ml chicken stock
2 tablespoons chopped fresh flat-leaf parsley
salt and freshly ground black pepper

**for the sweet and spicy tomato sauce**

1 tablespoon olive oil
1 onion, finely chopped
2 teaspoons garlic purée
2 tablespoons tomato purée
1 vegetable stock cube
1 bouquet garni
2 x 400 g cans chopped tomatoes
½ teaspoon dried oregano
100 ml red wine
½ teaspoon dried mint
juice of 1 lemon
1 tablespoon balsamic vinegar
1 tablespoon mild or hot chilli powder
2 tablespoons demerara sugar

1. Heat the oil for the sauce in a wide saucepan and gently cook the onion and garlic purée for 3–4 minutes until starting to soften. Add the tomato purée and cook for 1 minute, stirring. Stir in the remaining ingredients and bring to the boil. Gently simmer for 20 minutes until reduced, stirring occasionally. Check the seasoning, discard the bouquet garni and set aside.

2. Meanwhile, put the lentils in a pan of cold water and bring to the boil. Simmer for 5 minutes then drain and rinse. Set aside. Heat the oil in a heavy-based saucepan and cook the sausages for 5 minutes, turning until brown all over. Remove and set aside. Add the onions, garlic, carrots and rosemary sprig to the pan and cook for 8–10 minutes until starting to soften.

3. Return the sausages and lentils to the saucepan and pour in the stock and the sweet and spicy tomato sauce. Bring to the boil and simmer for 30 minutes until the lentils are tender and the sauce has thickened. Check the seasoning, sprinkle with the parsley and serve immediately.

Thanks to the likes of Marco Pierre White and Gordon Ramsay, pigs' trotters, a delicacy that I grew up with, have become a fashionable dish in recent years. As a young boy I used to watch my mother preparing pigs' trotters. Traditionally, trotters were regarded as poor man's food, but the intense flavour that you get from them was enough to make many a pauper feel well fed. The following recipe uses all the best bits from the trotters but serves them in a way that is less scary or offensive to many folk.

## TROTTER SPRING ROLLS

These crispy parcels are the perfect food for sharing with friends.

**serves 6**

4 pigs' trotters
700 g unsmoked gammon joint
6 tablespoons teriyaki sauce
1 tablespoon groundnut oil
½ onion, thinly sliced
2 carrots, cut into matchsticks
50 g mange tout, shredded
1 tablespoon caster sugar
12 x 15 g sheets filo pastry
75 g butter, melted
about 600 ml vegetable oil for deep frying
chilli sauce for dipping

1. Put the pigs' trotters and gammon into a large saucepan. Fill the pan with enough cold water to cover the meat. Bring to the boil and then reduce the heat and simmer very gently for 3 hours. Take off the heat and leave to cool in the pan.

2. When cool enough to handle, remove the trotters and gammon with a slotted spoon and transfer to a board. Discard the cooking liquid. Remove the skin from the trotters and shred the meat, discarding the bones, skin and gristle. Put into a large bowl. Remove the rind and fat from the gammon and shred the meat into bite-size pieces. Add to the trotter meat, stir in the teriyaki sauce and set aside.

3. Heat the groundnut oil in a large wok and stir fry the onion, carrots and mange tout for 3–4 minutes until starting to soften. Add the gammon and trotter meat and any leftover teriyaki sauce in the bottom of the bowl. Stir in the sugar and stir fry for 5 minutes, stirring until there is no liquid left in the wok. Remove and leave to cool.

4. Lay a sheet of filo pastry on a board. Place a large spoonful of the meat mixture near the end of one short side of the pastry. Brush the edges with melted butter, then fold over the sides and roll the spring roll up tightly, using a little melted butter to seal the flap. Repeat, to make 12 in total.

5. Heat a deep-fat fryer or put the oil into a large pan. Gently heat for 5 minutes or until it reaches 180°C and a cube of bread goes golden brown in 30 seconds. Carefully fry the spring rolls, one at a time, for 4 minutes each until golden brown. Drain on kitchen paper and keep warm in the oven while you cook the rest. Serve immediately with the chilli sauce to dip.

I couldn't leave French soil without treating myself to a meal at a local restaurant. With the aid of my French interpreter I was recommended a simple pork dish. It pains me to say this, but that meal was akin to falling in love. The dish was unpretentious yet sophisticated and confident enough to allow the pork to be centre of attention. This is my version of that dish and like all good love affairs the pork needs slow gentle cooking. So stick with it and perhaps you too will fall in love!

## STAR ANISE PORK BELLY

The slow cooking of the pork allows the layers of fat to simply melt away, producing an unbelievably tender meat.

**serves 4-6**

2 kg piece of pork belly
2 tablespoons sunflower oil
2 garlic bulbs, halved horizontally
4-5 fresh thyme sprigs
6 star anise
50 ml Pernod
50 ml white wine
450 ml chicken stock
salt and freshly ground black pepper

1. Preheat the oven to Gas Mark 3/160°C/fan oven 140°C. Lay the pork belly out flat on a board and score the skin evenly in a criss-cross pattern with a sharp knife (see tip). Then rub the skin all over with 1 tablespoon sunflower oil and seasoning.

2. Put the garlic halves cut side up, thyme sprigs and star anise in the base of a roasting tin. Lay the pork belly on top, skin side up, drizzle with the remaining oil and pour the Pernod around. Cover with foil and bake in the oven for 1½ hours.

3. Remove the pork from the oven and discard the foil. Baste with the pan juices and return to the oven, uncovered, for another 30-60 minutes, basting occasionally, until the pork is tender. Transfer the pork to a clean board.

4. Empty the juices from the roasting tin into a jug, reserving the garlic and discarding the thyme and star anise. Set aside. Increase the oven temperature to Gas Mark 7/220°C/fan oven 200°C. Return the pork belly to the roasting tin and cook in the oven for a further 20-30 minutes until the fat is golden and crispy. Remove the pork from the oven and put the meat on a clean board. Cover loosely with foil and leave to rest.

5. Spoon off any excess fat from the pork juices in the jug. Place the roasting tin on the hob and gently heat. Pour in the white wine, scraping the bottom of the tin with a wooden spoon, and bubble the liquid rapidly until reduced by half.

6. Add the chicken stock and garlic halves. Bring back to the boil and bubble for a further 5-8 minutes until reduced and thickened, squishing the garlic with the spoon. Strain the gravy through a fine sieve. Check the seasoning and keep warm. Carve the pork belly into large pieces and serve immediately with the gravy.

**tip** A clean and sharp Stanley knife (or craft knife) is the most effective tool for scoring the tough pork skin.

The French, like the British, love pork and it is used in a variety of ways. Pork is the most widely eaten meat in the world, providing almost 40 per cent of the world's protein intake. The great thing about it is that it can be eaten fresh or cured, making it a versatile meat, and almost every part of the pig can be consumed.

The pig is also one of most cost-effective animals to rear as almost every part of it is used in the food chain. But unlike other animals in the food chain pigs need a lot of looking after. Sheep and cattle can be pretty much left to their own devices but pigs need constant monitoring. I don't rear pigs on my farm because, with my constant travelling, I can't give them the time and attention they would need.

There is a misconception that pigs are very dirty animals, but this is far from the truth – in fact they are very clean. Even hour-old piglets somehow know to leave the nest to relieve themselves. And as for dirt, the reason they regularly roll in mud is because they do not have sweat glands; with no sweat to cool them they roll in mud to cool their skin. The layer of dried mud acts like a sun-block and protects their skin from the sun. Some pig farmers have been known to rub sunscreen on their pigs during very hot weather. So, far from being lazy and dirty, they're pretty smart creatures really.

A good pig farmer can achieve big litters from a sow – often between seven and twelve piglets – about twice a year. This is the minimum quantity that a pig farmer needs to achieve every time in order to be profitable, and for that to happen all the conditions have to be right. Despite appearances, pigs are easily stressed. You need to be a very special person, able to tune in to the needs of animals, to consider going into pig rearing.

One such person is Andrew Freemantle, whose empathy with his pigs I have watched in amazement. He treats them as if they are his children. Andrew is very knowledgeable about pigs and is an unsung hero of the pig world, well known in the south-west for running one of the best pig farms in the area. He is very hospitable, and Kenniford Farm at Clyst St Mary near Exeter is well worth a visit, as is his farm shop. In recent years he has branched out into providing hog roasts at special events. If you are planning a party or celebration with many guests, this is the ideal way to enjoy a really good meal. A spit roast may well be the only time that the consumer gets to see a half or a whole pig carcass. Carcasses are usually already dissected before sale, so here is a diagram and a list of the cuts and what they are best used for.

TROTTERS  Front and rear trotters or hocks can be cooked and eaten and are best stewed or braised. They are very gelatinous and are great for making stocks, soups and stews. Try Trotter Spring Rolls (page 178).

HAND AND SPRING  This is the lower part of the shoulder and the front legs. Cooking methods often include braising and roasting. It can also be cured on the bone and used to make cured or smoked ham, or sausages. See Toad in the Hole (page 183) for a great sausage recipe plus more.

LOIN  This is the top part of the pig, above the belly and the other side of the ribs. The loin can be cut into a pork loin joint or chops on or off the rib bones. Pork tenderloin fillet is found above the main loin joint and is the most tender and lean of all pork cuts. Try Sticky Pork Chops (page 172) or Milk-Braised Pork Loin with Chilli Crackling (page 174).

SPARE RIB JOINT  This is the main shoulder joint and contains the blade bone. Usually boned and rolled and often cured and made into collar bacon. See Roast Pork Shoulder with Cranberry and Rice Stuffing (page 183).

LEGS  These are the back legs of the pig that can be used for roasting or cut into leg steaks from the bone, but are more commonly known as hams. The whole leg is cured producing a wonderful ham, but can also be boned and then cured to make gammon. See Pineapple Glazed Ham (page 186).

BELLY  The pork belly is the underside of the pig, and can be used for steaks or diced for use in stews or casseroles. It is very popular in Chinese cooking – pork belly is used to make sweet and sour pork. It can be rolled for roasting or thinly sliced to make streaky bacon. See Star Anise Pork Belly (page 179) or The Black Farmer Cassoulet (page 173).

RIB  Taken from the pig's ribs above the belly and including the meat around the bones. Some uses include slow roasting and grilling. Try Ever So Sticky Ribs (page 172).

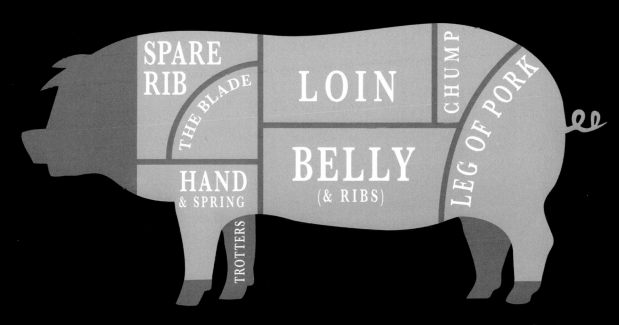

# TOAD IN THE HOLE

The secret to getting this to rise is to make sure the fat is really hot and that you pour the batter into the tin quickly, but carefully.

serves 4

30 g beef dripping
8 Black Farmer sausages
125 g self-raising flour
3 eggs
300 ml full fat milk
2 tablespoons snipped fresh chives
salt and freshly ground black pepper

for the guava sauce
4 tablespoons guava jam
125 ml white wine
juice of 2 limes
1 teaspoon Dijon mustard

1. Preheat the oven to Gas Mark 7/220°C/fan oven 200°C. Put the beef dripping into a roasting tin and put into the oven. When melted put the sausages into the tin, turning to coat. Cook in the oven for 10 minutes or until starting to brown.
2. Meanwhile, put the flour into a large bowl and make a well in the centre. Break the eggs into the well then, using an electric whisk, gradually whisk the eggs into the flour. Continue to whisk and gradually pour in the milk until a smooth batter is formed. Season with salt and black pepper and stir in the chives. Transfer to a jug and set aside.
3. Remove the roasting tin from the oven and quickly but carefully pour in the batter around the sausages. Return the tin to the oven and bake for 20–25 minutes until golden, puffed up and cooked.
4. Meanwhile, melt the guava jam in a small pan. Add the white wine and lime juice and bring to the boil. Simmer for 10 minutes until reduced. Season generously and stir in the mustard. Leave to cool while the sausages are cooking. Serve the toad in the hole drizzled with the guava sauce.

# ROAST PORK SHOULDER
## with Cranberry and Rice Stuffing

This is unbelievably tender. The pork fat helps to baste the pork from the inside, making it truly an amazing dish.

serves 6

250 g cooked long grain rice
75 g dried cranberries
½ teaspoon ground mace
20 freeze-dried curry leaves
3 tablespoons crunchy peanut butter
3 spring onions, finely chopped
1.75 kg boneless pork shoulder
salt and freshly ground black pepper

1. Preheat the oven to Gas Mark 5/190°C/fan oven 170°C. In a bowl mix together the rice, cranberries, mace, curry leaves, peanut butter and spring onions. Season with salt and black pepper and set aside.
2. Put the pork on a board and unroll. Cut the pork down the centre, leaving it still attached, and open out like a book. You may have to make a few horizontal cuts to open the pork out further and make it an even thickness.
3. Spoon the stuffing along the length of the pork, squidging it in place. Re-roll the pork and tie securely in five or six places. Place in a roasting tin and cover with foil. Roast in the oven for 2 hours
4. Remove the foil from the pork and continue to roast for a further 1 hour 15 minutes until browned and the pork is cooked. Remove from the roasting tin, cover with foil and leave to rest for 15 minutes before carving in thick slices.

The fantastic thing about pork is that it can be cured to produce the most wonderful gammons and hams. Long gone are the days of heavily salted brines – the British have definitely got it right when it comes to curing. Ham is the great staple convenience meat. For generations it was served as a meal that could be eaten anywhere away from the home. Ham has staved off hunger pangs for generations and even today millions of ham sandwiches are made to be eaten on the go. Unfortunately, people don't cook ham like they used to and more often than not ham is only made at home on special occasions.

## PINEAPPLE GLAZED HAM

If you want to use a gammon on the bone, then weigh the joint and recalculate the cooking time in the tropical juice at 45 minutes per 500 g.

**serves 12**

**2.5 kg boneless smoked gammon joint**
**1 litre fresh tropical juice**
**5 tablespoons pineapple jam**

1. Put the gammon in a large saucepan and cover with the tropical juice and 500 ml water. You may need to top up the pan with a little more water to ensure the gammon is just covered. Bring to the boil, then cover and simmer gently for 2½ hours or until cooked. Leave to cool in the cooking liquid.

2. Preheat the oven to Gas Mark 7/220°C/fan oven 200°C. Mix the jam with 2 tablespoons of reserved cooled cooking liquid and then sieve until smooth. Put the jam mixture into a pan and bring to the boil. Simmer for 3–4 minutes until thickened.

3. Remove the skin from the gammon, leaving a thin layer of fat, and score with a sharp knife in a criss-cross pattern. Spread the pineapple glaze over the fat, reserving a little for later. Line a roasting tin with foil and roast in the oven for 20 minutes until caramelized. Brush over the rest of the glaze and leave to stand for 10 minutes, then carve or leave to get cold and keep in the fridge until needed.

' I make this recipe every Christmas. When I cook this I start with a very large ham joint deliberately because I love the idea of being able to go to the fridge and cut off a slice whenever it takes my fancy. '

The five senses that we have – seeing, hearing, feeling, smelling and tasting – all must work as one for us to enjoy our food. With most other things in life we can get by without these senses working in unison. Food needs all the senses to be synchronized for us to get pleasure from what we eat. Food has been such a fundamental part of our being since time immemorial that there are many rituals that surround its consumption. Living in the West we take plentiful food for granted, and I believe that here in the UK we have an incredibly wide variety of food choices available to us, much more so than our European neighbours who tend to stick with their own traditional dishes.

For me, food has been my chosen vehicle to recount my story of how I became The Black Farmer. Cooking offers me an opportunity to relax and bring out my creativity. I enjoy the

challenge of trying to create a dish out of ingredients that I happen to have at hand and this I have found enables me not to be trapped by convention. From this was born the idea of 'Flavours without Frontiers'. To achieve this you need to clear your mind of any preconceptions of how things should be done and trust your senses.

When I started this book I promised myself I would celebrate its completion by taking a well-earned holiday in Portugal, and I am now only a week away from cruising the food markets of that country. I am also planning to cook a thank-you dish for family and friends who have helped me in the process of writing. Unfortunately it will be only a small affair, so for those of you who will not be invited the best I can offer in consolation are all the recipes in this book. I hope you enjoy them as much as I do.